Life's Chrysalis

Stories of Transformation and the Power of Change

Compiled by
Monica Kunzekweguta

Authors Without Boundaries – a division of Prime Mind Publishing

admin@authorswithoutboundaries.net

www.authorswithoutboundaries.net

Published: Alberta, Canada

Book Cover: Authors Without Boundaries (AWB), Canada

First Printing 2019

First Edition 2019

10 9 8 7 6 5 4 3 2 1

Prime Mind Publishing House was established by authors who saw the need to pool resources together to support others still facing challenges in breaking into the market. The ultimate vision was to publish stories that have a real impact on people's lives. Most of these authors had already established themselves in the business of writing. However, what brought them together was the realization that the pen could be used to inspire, encourage, and empower others. As a publishing house, Prime Mind is the home to Authors Without Boundaries (AWB). AWB is a consortium of independent authors who come together to collaborate on various literary pieces of work. Comprising of budding and professional writers, this group, strives to assist each member in attaining par excellence. The authors operate from all continents on the globe and are a true "rainbow nation." 2017 promises to be yet another "Best Seller" year. We look forward in anticipation!

Table of Contents

Legal Disclaimer

The information and content within this book, Life's Chrysalis 13 Stories of Transformation and the Power of Change is not a substitute for any form of professional counseling such as a Counselor, Life Coach, Psychologist or Physician. The contents and information provided do not constitute professional or legal advice in any way, shape or form. The advice contained herein is not meant to replace the professional role of a psychologist or any of these professionals.

All chapters are written at the discretion of and with the full accountability of each author. Monica Kunzekweguta, Authors Without Boundaries or Prime Mind (Print Media for Development), are not responsible or liable for any of the specific details, description of people, places or things, personal interpretations, experiences, stories, and narratives contained within. The compiler and publisher are not liable for any misrepresentations, false or unknown statements, actions, or judgments made by any or their chapter content in this book. Each writer is responsible for their contribution and has shared their story in good faith to help others.

The information offered in this book is only intended to be for general information about general life issues. You are under no obligation to use it.

Any decision you make and the outcomes thereof are entirely your own doing. Under no circumstances can you hold the compiler Monica Kunzekweguta, Authors Without Boundaries or Prime Mind (Print Media for Development) liable for any loss or expenses incurred by you, as a result of materials, advice, coaching or mentoring suggested within. You should not use any of the information offered without first seeking legal and other professional advice.

Foreword

This whole project, compiling the 13 stories was incredible. It was a great vision by the compiler, Monica Kunzekweguta. Reading from her biography, it is obvious she believes in the power of storytelling. She is encouraging ordinary people across the globe to share their life experiences through writing and as a result, influencing others to transform.

Hard times come to every life.

Not everyone experiences transformation.

What is there about some people that cause them to not only survive but to transform?

You are holding such 13 stories of transformation. Every story is as unique as the soul who is living it. Each one is precious.

The author of the first story, Farai Rukunda, is a friend of mine. I'll always remember the first time I saw him and heard him speak. He could not stop smiling. Since there was nothing particularly remarkable about the day, his joy gave me the impression of someone who probably grew up with every advantage.

Then one day he told me about this book, and what the experience was like for him the morning he began to write his story. There was something about the look in his eyes, and the way the urge to write came to him, that I needed to hear.

So, it felt like I was handed a rare gift when he first shared the stories you are about to read. I imagined the courage it took for each writer to get to the page. How many tears fell as real moments were relived? How much trust did it take to become vulnerable again, like a small child who knows nothing other than to be completely open and honest? What epiphanies, big and small, came to each writer?

Recently, I asked Farai what he most hopes will happen from the publication of these stories. He smiled, of course, as if he has already seen a vision of what can be. You'll want to read on and hear his answer for yourself.

You also get to decide for yourself just how transformation came to be for all these courageous authors. What matters for now is this…It *has.*

Which means transformation could also happen for any one of us, for our world, at any time.

Ellen Moore

Bridgewater Consultants

Saint Joseph, Michigan

www.bridgewaterc.com

Acknowledgments

I would like to express appreciations and gratitude to my co-authors, thank you for entrusting me with your personal stories and an opportunity to personally work with each of you. Your dedication and discipline provide a model to encourage us to live better lives.

Our book is a powerful masterpiece for which I am truly grateful. It is so much harder to do things on our own, so this collaborative effort will mean your "Stories of transformation and the power of change", will help our readers to seek their growth and a renewal of the mind. Some of you were writing for the first time; you decided to bear it all so that you can help another person work out how to navigate this venture called life. All of you inspire me because you encourage me to continue compiling stories and transform lives one chapter at a time.

Many others need to be acknowledged. Therefore I begin with the people who gave me my foundation, parents and the whole family; you instilled strong values that helps me to stay balanced and grounded in my day-to-day activities.

To everyone who has made this journey enjoyable and productive, thank you. Tasha Brown, your dedication and support has paid off.

Introduction

Transformation is defined as a marked change in form, nature, appearance, expression or altering the very nature of something. It is often viewed as difficult, but it is a natural process which involves changing your thoughts and how you communicate to self. Unless we share our stories, we will not change situations, touch, move or inspire anyone. Our stories have a purpose.

In this book, you will read true personal, stories from authors across the globe sharing their life experiences and how it has impacted their lives and people around them. Among these authors, for some, it is their very first time writing a story and participating in an Anthology. We hope their stories are the first of many to come and we look forward to their partnership with us in the future.

There are 13 very different stories from authors sharing their personal life experiences. Some of these stories have led the authors to go through total **Personal Transformation.** Among these stories there are those which are very emotional and heartbreaking but, in the end, they are true testimonials of new hope and resilience. Because of these individuals' painful life experiences, they were the fortunate ones who were able to find inner peace and healing. Today they are helping others who have traveled similar journeys to heal and move on with their lives.

You will also read stories where you find people who have witnessed **Transformation in others** and how it has positively impacted them. Sometimes we observe people around us changing in behavior, outlook to life and many other ways. Those changes can be contagious and end up influencing others to transform.

Many times, people always wonder or fail to identify their purpose on this earth or sometimes it is not entirely clear. In this book, there are fascinating and amazing stories where there were terrible beginnings, and through life experiences, hope and miracles were born. Sometimes as we travel this life journey, our real "Calling" becomes more evident, and this leads us to **Transformation through your calling.**

When you let your guard down, there is finally room for something different to transpire, something unexpected...Life's Chrysalis. People often talk about wanting to make a change in their life, but they put it off, or they are afraid to take the first step.

The following are a few quotations extracted from some of the stories you are about to read,

"Rejection sheds off all the things you think you should be and leaves only who you are."

"There are certain life experiences you just don't talk about..."

"I became an orphan at six years old."

"This frightening reality murders the child in me..."

"I lowered my standards, and it was the worst mistake I ever made."

Reading these stories will have you saying "Yes!" to change,

"Yes!" to taking that first step, "Yes!" to discovering your calling. There is a new path before you.

Do not be defined by your past; transform into who you are meant to be!

Just remember that every successful person has gone through Transformation. We hope there is a story which will directly speak to you and bring growth and positive change in your life.

Hello Ardié

Thank you for Supporting Living Beyond Hope projects. Your help goes a long way! Together we are touching lives.

With much love

Farai [illegible]

Living Beyond Hope

By Farai Rukunda

Life definitely is a journey which is molded by our life experiences, by the people surrounding us, our environment in general and our spiritual state of mind. I became an orphan at six years old. I grew up in Zimbabwe Africa, an environment where I experienced conditional love, in some cases unconditional love, feelings of abandonment, and at times moments of uncertainty. Forty-two years later I find myself residing in Stevensville Michigan, U.S.A, married with six children. Today I can say everything I had hoped for in life has been given to me, education and family. It took forty years of my life to discover, that time had come to live beyond everything I had hoped for. My life journey has had its ups and downs. Through it all, I believe God is honestly using me as His vessel to touch hundreds of lives in my home village of Arnoldine Mission. The journey to get to this juncture has not been easy.

God cries with you in times of tragedy

On the afternoon on March 24th, 1976, I remember playing outside as a little boy when two ladies (neighbors of ours), stopped by our house in a small township of Kambuzuma, an African township in Salisbury (now Harare), the capital. They went inside our home. Shortly after that, I saw my sister Rhoda and my Aunt Beulah run out of the house, crying hysterically in disbelief and running up the street away from our house. My sister Winnie was sobbing uncontrollably as well but had stayed back with me. There was confusion at the house. Soon enough, I learned the reason for the tears and fear I witnessed—my parents Lovemore and Mary Rukunda were in an accident. They had just left the house and were on their motorcycle when a drunk driver ran into them, killing them instantly.

My six-year-old mind did not understand why people were so upset and why they could not stop sobbing. I was baffled. Death to me at that time was meaningless. I had no idea what had just happened, and I had no clue what that would mean from that day forward. I remember laughing at my sister, Winnie, wondering why she was continuing to cry.

Forty years later, living in Stevensville Michigan, I felt the need to revisit this day, but I was not sure why? On one early Saturday morning in February of 2016, I had gone in to work for a few hours when I decided to call my eldest sister Rhoda, who lives in Sharon Massachusetts. The purpose of my call was to find out about the details of the events on March 24th, 1976. I had never asked anybody about the circumstances of my parents' death. I had accepted the facts as they were back then and moved on. Maybe I was afraid to find out about the truth.

As I talked to Rhoda on the phone, I was pacing back and forth at my office. There were no other employees present since it was a weekend. The only noise I could hear was the buzzing sound of all the sophisticated scientific instruments in the building.

Rhoda, without asking any questions, explained the sequence of events that day. I asked her the question I had never asked before—if she saw our parents at the scene of the accident. Rhoda told me that she remembered that day very well. She said upon arrival at the site of the accident; she saw two bodies lying on the ground covered with blankets. Rhoda first uncovered my father as she saw him lying there with the socks she recognized very well. She then proceeded to my mother who was lying a few feet away and uncovered her as well.

As I listened to her telling me these details, I felt like my body had just frozen into a block of ice and fear had invaded my soul. I realized at that moment; I had been suppressing all thoughts about what happened on March 24th, 1976 for the past forty years. I am sure if you talked to anybody who was present at my parents' funeral, they would remember five children—Rhoda (nineteen), Tsitsi (sixteen), Winnie (eight), Carol (four) and me at age six—left behind with what seemed to be a hopeless future.

God continues to bless you always

Through the grace of God, my parents had forged a strong bond with two missionaries, Norman and Winnie Thomas who came to Arnoldine (my home village) in 1964. That bond started when my mother Mary helped provide care for Norman and Winnie's children as they were busy doing mission work at Arnoldine and in the country. Over the years in the 1960s my mother grew so close to the Thomas's that she became family.

Unfortunately, Norman and Winnie were declared prohibited immigrants by the white regime in 1973. They were not allowed to come back into the country because they were supporting the elimination of segregation between whites and blacks.

They moved to Zambia where they continued God's work but eventually returned to the United States. After my parent's death, Norman and Winnie, along with my aunts and uncles, shared the responsibilities to provide social welfare for my siblings and I. Norman and Winnie were not allowed to return to Zimbabwe at the time but they were supporting us financially and through letter correspondence.

I remember, soon after my parents were buried, there were still many family members lingering around at Arnoldine village. I remembered my older sister Tsitsi gathering my two sisters Winnie, Carol and I and told us that from that day forward our aunt Beulah was going to take the role of being our mother. The transition was abrupt, and no one talked about the death of our parents anymore. I was very confused, and I felt very insecure and lonely. It felt like I had been abandoned in the wilderness and had nowhere to go. I was searching for love and protection so much that I was scared! I had so many unanswered questions, but I did not know how to ask them. In the years that followed, my auntie Beulah gave it her best to provide unwavering love and support to us and to this day I am very grateful.

My grandmother, Lois Mbwizhu played a pivotal role in keeping the entire family clan glued together and staying focused. My grandmother was a very strong-willed individual. She was energetic, spiritual and very vocal. On school holidays she used to wake us up at 4 am to go to the cornfields to work. That was a harrowing experience, but over the years we got used to it. I can honestly say today; I am a morning person because of her. It took years way into my adulthood to make the connection. I believe people are more productive early in the morning when there is no distraction. Ironically enough, as I am writing this paragraph, it is 4:20 am Tuesday, October 9th, 2018. I am forever grateful to my grandmother for instilling good work ethics in me.

Many other aunts and uncles were very influential in my life, and I am very thankful for their support. I learned later over the years that after my parents' death the family decided it was utterly crucial that my siblings and I were kept together in one home so we could grow together. Looking back through the years, I am very grateful for their well thought out decisions.

My aunt Beaula and her siblings worked the best they could to nurture and guide us as we grew up. Their love and support will always be cherished.

I lived in Zimbabwe up to the age of eighteen years. In August 1988 Norman and Winnie assisted me in coming to the United States to further my education. I remember just a few days before I departed for the USA, I had gone to say goodbye to my grandmother Lois Mbwizhu and other family members at Arnoldine. It was in early August of 1988; my grandmother and I were sitting in the sun in the middle of a cornfield, and she was telling me the history of my parents. She was also telling me never to forget my roots. I remember this day very vividly; my grandmother was smart. She knew I was about to embark on a journey 10,000 miles across the Atlantic Ocean to reunite with the Thomas's and further my education. She also knew there was a possibility of me never coming back and I believe that was why we were having that long conversation.

Even though my siblings and I had lost both our parents, we were blessed with another set of parents who understood our culture and had a special bond with our biological parents long before I even came into this world. I never really knew my biological parents, but I can say the parents I know today are Norman and Winnie Thomas.

Fighting Gods call

Fast forward many years. I achieved my college education at Wright State University. I am married to my wife Rutendo, and we have six children (5 boys and the youngest is a girl), Tendai (Twenty-Seven), Taurai (Twenty-Three), Tatenda (Nineteen), Tadiwanashe (Eighteen), Tafara (Fifteen) and Tafadzwa (Five). My family and I currently live in Stevensville Michigan, and I manage a group of engineers at LECO Corporation, a laboratory equipment manufacturing company.

In January of 2013 I received a phone call from my Dad (Norman) wishing me a 'Happy New Year,' but most importantly he asked me if I could go with him back to Zimbabwe and visit my home village, Arnoldine. Without even thinking about it I refused the request, but I promised to go with him the following year, 2014.

A year went by, and 2014 arrived very quickly. I received a call again from my dad on January 1st wishing me a 'Happy New Year' but most importantly following up on my last promise to him to travel to Zimbabwe together. I responded to him thoughtfully that time, but my answer was still a no. I told him the trip was going to be too expensive and I could not afford it, so that was the end of the discussion.

A week later my dad called again offering to pay for the trip. I was very appreciative of the offer, but the answer was still no due to my not having enough vacation time from work. That time he did not take no for an answer. Instead he insisted I should attempt to ask my company if they could make an exception for me to go. I was convinced the company would refuse that request, but after talking to management, they thought that it would be an extraordinary trip. Without hesitation, they permitted me to go with no strings attached. I was shocked to hear their reaction, but I continued to search for a reason not to go.

I came home that evening and explained to my wife what had transpired, and I asked her whether I should still travel with my dad. She stared at me for a few seconds and said, "I think you are a very stupid individual." I was shocked to hear her say that to me, but I knew then it was time to stop giving excuses why I could not make the trip. It was at this point I thought I should concede and let my father know I was ready to go. He was very excited when I told him I would travel with him back to my home village. Within four hours of our conversation, the trip was booked, and we were scheduled to leave for Zimbabwe in early August 2014.

As the days approached to travel back to Zimbabwe, I was increasingly anxious and nervous because I did not want to go. The night before the trip my family drove me to Chicago to spend the night there since I was catching my flight at Midway Airport early in the morning.

Well, the morning of the departure things did not go well. I overslept and missed my flight. After a long morning of regret, guilt, tears, and frustration I knew I had let my dad down and I knew one way or another I had to get to Zimbabwe and meet with him.

Beginning of Transformation....

As you can tell from this chapter thus far, I had been trying to find every reason not to go to Zimbabwe and visit my home village. Two years in a row I had been resisting to take this trip coming up with one excuse after another. Up to now, I am still not quite sure why I was not enthusiastic about the trip. Every reason I came up with for not going, God knocked it out of the way.

However, when I finally missed my flight, I now had a good reason for not going, considering there was going to be extra cost involved in rebooking the airline ticket. In retrospect, God had finally given me the reason not to go. Surprisingly enough I found myself frantically attempting to make every arrangement possible to get on the next flight to Zimbabwe.

Out of desperation, I called my mom, Winnie, seeking assistance with rebooking for the next earliest flight to Zimbabwe. In our conversation, she said, "Farai, do you have to go to Zimbabwe? Norm is a big boy; he can be in Zimbabwe without you." In my response, I told Winnie that the trip was significant to me, and I must go. We finally both came to an understanding and without delay Winnie managed to arrange another flight on my behalf for the next day. I was very thankful and relieved. The next day I was up bright and early, I was on time at the airport, and I finally departed for Zimbabwe.

When we have the Ah ha! Moment life starts to become more meaningful

My flight was uneventful, and I traveled well. I met with my father and his second wife, Mae Gautier, and began making arrangements for how we were going to spend our time. The priority was traveling to Arnoldine mission, but along the way, we made several stops in different villages visiting my relatives and paying our respects to those who had passed on.

Eventually, we arrived at Arnoldine. We were received by so many family members and close friends; Norman was reunited with many friends he had worked with 50+ years ago. It was amazing to witness my dad reuniting with members of the community whom he served back in the missionary days.

We spent the night at Arnoldine. During the stay, we toured the village meeting with family members and friends. We toured the clinic which was started by Winnie Thomas with financial help from a United Methodist church in Birmingham Michigan. We visited the new secondary school (it started in 2013 with seven students), which was a small building divided into four small classrooms. The secondary school was using this building as a temporary space as they sought help to construct an appropriate classroom.

As we were touring all these places, it was amazing to learn of all Norman and Winnie's accomplishments 50+ years ago. Those accomplishments were still making a positive impact on the community. Everyone in Arnoldine knew of the Thomas's and all their accomplishments. The clinic which was started by Winnie had become the central healthcare center supporting Arnoldine community and the neighboring villages. I could not believe that even at age eighty-two Norman Thomas still had an interest in seeing the development of the Arnoldine secondary school.

The last place we visited was my parents' gravesite. We arrived there, and Norman cried continuously as he remembered my parents. We hugged and wept together as we were standing in front of the graves. I was overwhelmed by emotions. We prayed and returned to my Uncle Lovemore Mbwizhu's house in preparation for our departure. At that point, my mind was beginning to process the whole visit. It was mind-boggling for me to learn of the work Norman and Winnie had done and to see the positive impact still existing fifty years later.

As we were getting ready to leave, I started having lots of questions in my mind. What was my purpose in life? Why was I there? It took my dad two years to convince me to visit my home village with him and his wife, Mae Gautier. Was this just a trip he wanted to do or was God speaking to him? I had no answers, but my mind was racing.

As I was getting ready to get into the car to begin our journey back to the capital city of Zimbabwe, Harare, my cousin Brian Mbwizhu approached me and asked, "We would like to ask you for your help?"

The first thing which came into my mind as I heard that question was, okay what do you want? Money? However, I did not express those thoughts out loud, but instead, I waited for him to tell me what help he needed. He then said, "Could you please help us paint our church?" That was not the request I was expecting. I was humbled. I told Brian to send me the quote for painting the church once I return to the USA. At that point, after witnessing all the testimonies by the community regarding work which had been done by the Thomas's, I was ready to commit myself to help them paint the church even if it meant money was coming out of my pocket. The Zimbabwe trip transformed me. After all my resistance to going to Zimbabwe, I have to say it with certainty that it was well worth it.

God using me as His vessel to begin life-changing projects at Arnoldin:

I returned to Michigan with lots of emotions from my Zimbabwe trip experience. I was feeling grateful to all my family members and LECO

Corporation who supported me to make the trip a success. I was ready to help my Arnoldine village at whatever the cost. Shortly after my return, I received a message from Brian (my cousin who had requested help to paint the church). The cost of painting the church was $700. As a Stevensville United Methodist church member and Chairperson of its Administrative Council, I came back from Zimbabwe ready to serve in whatever way God wanted me to.

Tuesday, September 26th, 2014, we had the church's Administrative Council meeting, and everything seemed normal during the meeting until towards the end. Ms. Carolyn Yoder, who was in charge of Missions at the time had nothing to report for September, but she was seeking ideas from the Administrative Council on any mission projects to support. When I heard her request seeking ideas for mission projects to support, I could not believe what I was hearing. That was another reminder for me to know God was guiding that whole process. No one had any ideas, so I finally said it! "My home village of Arnoldine Mission was looking for help painting their church." There was silence for a few seconds and Pastor Gordie Barry (Stevensville United Methodist Church's pastor at the time) said, "Let's do it." The Administrative Council board unanimously agreed, and help was on the way. They provided $1,200 for the painting, and that money was sent right away. Thank you to Stevensville United Methodist congregation for your generosity and support.

Within two weeks of sending the money to Arnoldine, I received the before and after pictures of the Arnoldine church. The church looked brand new, and it was beautiful. It was amazing to see the before and after photos. That church had not been painted in thirty years. The project was completed and a success!!! I presented the work to the congregation of Stevensville United Methodist Church, and they were delighted to learn of the progress.

The Beginning of Living Beyond Hope, a registered 501c-3 Organization

A few days after I presented the work which was being done at Arnoldine, I received a call from Pastor Gordie Barry requesting to meet for lunch that day. I was not sure what that meeting request was all about, but I accepted the invitation. We met for lunch at the Lake House restaurant on Hilltop road in St. Joseph, Michigan, and his first question was, "What else does the village of Arnoldine need?" I stared at him in disbelief. Then I asked, "Do you want the long list or the short list? He replied, "Just tell me." I told him the school children did not have clean water and they were walking two miles round trip every morning fetching dirty water from a stream. The kids did not have textbooks, nor did they have desks and chairs in the classroom. Lastly, I told him they needed more classroom space.

At our next Administrative Council Meeting, Pastor Gordie Barry proposed that the Stevensville congregation become the sister church with Arnoldine United Methodist Church. He also proposed to the board that we raise money to provide more help to the Arnoldine community. The board unanimously accepted the proposal. The church began fundraising and started funding the projects. We started with clean water, followed by books then desks. It was at that point in July of 2015 when Pastor Gordie Barry retired.

I was worried not knowing what the new incoming pastor, David Hills, was going to do. I knew we had more work to do, but I was not sure of Pastor Hills' vision for the church. Pastor Hills adopted the idea of uplifting the quality of life at Arnoldine, but he was not comfortable having the church continue to funnel the money for Arnoldine projects from outside the church donors. Instead, he suggested opening a 501c-3 organization.

At that point in the game, I already realized I had become an agent for God to improve lives at Arnoldine Mission. I had begun to feel the pressure to fulfill the plans we had outlined with Pastor Gordie Barry before his departure. I was scared because I knew this project was picking up a life of its own. I prayed about it and told myself, many unexplainable events had happened on this journey, and the only explanation I had was God was guiding us!!

I started looking for board members for the organization. I knew I needed team members with different skills to contribute to the organization. We would need persons who would bring communication skills, knowledge about non-profit organizations, knowledge about social media and someone gifted in organizing fundraising events. Well, thank God, I was able to find those members, and they were willing to join the team. On January 27, 2018, Living Beyond Hope, was legally registered as a 501c-3 organization. We are very thankful to SCORE, a nonprofit organization which assists the entrepreneur dreaming of beginning her or his small business. Their guidance and support during the 501c-3 registration process were phenomenal.

On April 27th, 2018, Living Beyond Hope launched its new website, www.livingbeyondh.com, special thank you to our web designer Mr. Hunter Willis. On that same day, Living Beyond Hope held its first Fundraiser as a registered 501c-3 nonprofit organization. That evening we raised $6,000 in 2 hours, special thank you to the local businesses, volunteers and community who came out to support such an important event.

Living beyond ourselves

As I mentioned at the beginning my this story, growing up in Zimbabwe, I experienced both unconditional and conditional love, abandonment, resilience, and countless other emotions, but as hopeless as the situation seemed I still believed there was hope. If nothing else I told myself I should rely on God and no matter the circumstances education was going to be my gate to success.

My life journey taught me many lessons. Among them I learned:

- God is patient
- God is always forgiving and kind
- Even when we are at the darkest times in our lives, God cries with us and also blesses us along the way
- God works through people to impact lives
- God talks to us all the time; we must pay attention
- God is with us all the time
- Forgive because anger can be cancerous and not healthy for any soul.

With no doubt, God worked through Norman Thomas to convince me to go to Arnoldine with him and Mae Gautier in August of 2014. That trip transformed my life, and today my focus in life is to make a difference in people's lives. Living Beyond Hope Organization certainly provides the platform to make a difference in the lives of children at Arnoldine Secondary school.

As I grew up, I always hoped that I would get married and have a family. I always hoped I would have an opportunity to get an education and be successful. Today I can say, that through the grace of God I have achieved all those goals. Does this make me free of problems? Absolutely not! But what I have hoped for God gave to me, and today I have to *live beyond that hope,* and it is time to serve others.

Feelings of Gratitude

I have so much gratitude for the Stevensville United Methodist congregation. If it were not for the congregation which stepped up to fund the initial projects at Arnoldine Mission Center, Living Beyond Hope would not be in existence today. I am also thankful to the LBH board members, Ms. Maria Hutchins of LECO Corporation, Ms. Veronica Jackson of LECO Corporation, Mr. Jesse Robins of Stevensville

United Methodist Church, Ms., Rachel Wade of United Way and Ms. Ashley Horn of Stevensville United Methodist church. These board members, bring so much talent to the organization, and they are indeed a blessing.

Behind the scene were other local private companies, organizations, and volunteers who worked hard to jump start our organization. Special thank you to Benton Harbor Sunrise Rotary Club, which has been supportive and continues to do so, E-Tech com Corporation and Mr. Tim Judkins of LECO Corporation for all their efforts in generating 3D models for the classrooms and teachers' cottages. These models were important for visual purposes to potential donors.

Last but not least, I am very grateful for my family. My wife Tendi and children Tendai, Taurai, Tatenda, Tadiwanashe, Tafara, and Tafadzwa have been my rock!! They have been my cheer leaders behind the scene and a strong pillar of support. I am very grateful to have them in my corner as Living Beyond Hope organization travels to new heights.

Farai Rukunda

Farai Rukunda is the founder and visionary of Living Beyond Hope. A native of Zimbabwe, Africa. Farai migrated to the United States in 1988 to further his education, obtaining a Master's of Science in Biochemistry and a Bachelor's of Science in Biology/Chemistry from Wright State University. After working at Wright State University as a Senior Research Scientist in the Department of Chemistry for 15 years, he moved to Southwestern, Michigan in 2007 to work for LECO Corporation, a global manufacturer of laboratory equipment. In his current role, Farai oversees a group of Technical and Field service engineers for the Separation Science product line, supporting customers throughout the United States and managing daily projects by being the conduit between customers and the company.

Farai is also a member of the Stevensville United Methodist Church where he serves the role of being the Chairperson for the Administrative Council, and a member of the Benton Harbor Sun Rise Rotary Club.
Contact Farai:

www.Livingbeyondh.com

livingbeyondh@gmail.com

http://bit.ly/2DZYYk4

Displacement & Reinvention

By Tendai Masiya

I was born and raised in Dangamvura, a suburb in the city of Mutare, Zimbabwe. I am the second born in a family of three boys and two girls. I attended Sheni Primary School in Dangamvura and my years in primary school were the best years Zimbabwe ever experienced as a nation. When I started school, Zimbabwe was three years old having recently been born in 1980. There was a great sense of euphoria in the country and even as a young person I could sense the excitement. We were told stories of heroism displayed by the freedom fighters in fighting for our independence and not to take this independence for granted. Every day on the 8 o'clock news bulletins (TV prime time evening national news) we would watch the news of a beaming and radiant new Prime Minister Robert Mugabe exuding confidence and polished English talking to other world leaders and journalists.

My parents also shared with me how life was in Zimbabwe, then Rhodesia before 1980. They were not allowed to go in certain parts of the city due to racial policies at that time. I felt lucky then; I could go anywhere with my parents without problems or restrictions. I was very thankful to the freedom fighters. During the early 1980s, my mother was working at Grindlay's Bank in the city center of Mutare, and she was still young having migrated from the rural areas of Sharara in Rusape to seek a better life in the city. My father had grown up in Biriiri in Chimanimani, and he would tell me how intelligent he was because he attended Goromonzi High School and passed his GCSE Ordinary Level Cambridge Examinations in 1953. He would share that, 'some of the government cabinet officials (Ministers) and Judges you are seeing in independent Zimbabwe were some of my classmates at Goromonzi.' I would marvel at hearing him talk about people I was now seeing on television were his classmates. Listening to him made me wonder why he was not as successful as his former classmates.

Furthermore, I thought to myself, if he had become successful and became a Minister maybe our life could have been better off. Perhaps to the extent of being able to afford living in low-density suburbs such as Borrowdale, Highlands among others instead of Dangamvura, a low-income high-density neighborhood. My father then told me a story when he was awarded a scholarship to go to the United States of America but turned it down, since he was in a serious relationship with a girlfriend at the time. I wondered if he had gone to America, would I have been born? It was good those days to be a young boy, and Zimbabwe was a doyen of hope that everything was possible.

Life was good during this era, and family life was a close-knit and parents in my neighborhood could discipline any child for being naughty. When I started grade 1 my sister, who is the firstborn of the family was doing her grade 7 at Sheni primary school. During break time she would come and pick me from my class to spend some time in her class. As a young boy, I used to be intimidated by the big boys and girls in her class. My sister would give me the confidence not to worry, but she was only with me at the Sheni primary school for a short period. My sister successfully finished her grade 7 and was accepted to attend her secondary education (high school) at St. Augustine's secondary school which was a boarding school in Penhalonga. I was very sad as I witnessed my sister transitioning from our primary school to secondary school. I no longer had a sister or brother in primary school to look up to. My sister would be gone months at a time at the boarding school. However, she would come back home on school breaks and stay for a few weeks before returning to school. I used to cry the day my sister would leave home to go to boarding school. I would go to my bedroom, lock myself and sob uncontrollably thinking I won't see her again. Life moved fast, and as years passed, I developed new friendships in school and could now stand on my own.

The primary school years passed rapidly, and my outlook on life was changing at a fast pace. During that time Mutare was a bustling city and used to be flooded by Mozambican nationals who were running away from RENAMO activities in their country, seeking refuge in Zimbabwe. RENAMO was a militant organization and political movement which was being sponsored by a foreign country. It was founded in 1975 as part of an anti-communist backlash against the country's ruling FRELIMO party. I used to meet many Mozambicans in the city center, and some of them worked as domestic workers or garden boys (males who work around the yard in residential areas) in our neighborhoods. They would share with us how the war was ravaging their country and how the leader of RENAMO, Matsangaissa was a dissident force, bend on destabilizing their independence. Majority of people in my neighborhood and the city at large were xenophobic towards Mozambicans. We had a superiority complex because we had good homes, infrastructure and quality of life that gave us a false sense of superiority. At that young age, I didn't have a clear grasp of the political struggles in Mozambique. I did not understand why Mozambicans could run away from their country leaving relatives and loved ones. I just imagined it was difficult for them, the same way it was for me when I could not cope when my sister was away for four months at boarding school, let alone years. The Mozambicans in my neighborhood were hard working and would do any work which the locals wouldn't do like selling candy and cigarette on street corners and working the fields for extra cash. The Zimbabwean citizens mistreated the Mozambicans, and I would see some crying after being rounded by immigration officers in the city center of Mutare being liable for deportation.

I completed my grade 7 successfully, and I was accepted to St. Augustine's secondary school, the same boarding school my sister had attended. I had also been accepted at St Dominic's High School, a local commuter school in Mutare. My parents preferred for me to go to St. Augustine's boarding school, but I did not share the same sentiment. I wanted to go to St. Dominic High school that way I would be with my parents all the time. However, my parents did not entertain that idea. Their word carried weight, so I had to attend St. Augustine's Mission School instead of St Dominic's High School in Mutare.

When I went to St. Augustine's it meant that most of my time was now being spent in a secluded boarding school in Penhalonga. At this place, I met different young people from around the country, unlike my local primary school where I schooled with locals only. Life at the boarding school was a significant change for me. During the first days at the beginning of each school term, I would cry because I was missing my parents I had left at home. As days, months and years progressed I started making friends at my new school and experienced new life which meant that I gained more confidence to do things without asking parents to do it for me. By the time I completed high school I was more independent and would go back to our home for holidays with a sense of superiority complex to my former primary school classmates who had remained local for their high school education. I was now more aware that the world did not start and end in my city.

I acquired decent grades in my GCE Advanced Level examinations and was accepted at the University of Zimbabwe to pursue a Bachelor of Arts degree with a major in Philosophy and History and a minor in Sociology in March of 1997. I was excited at the new prospect of attending a nationally recognized university. During my orientation week, I was politicized about national issues by young upcoming leaders at the university who were activists voicing their grievances and opinions against the government. It did not take long before I joined them to become an activist, which landed me in trouble a few times. When I attended boarding school, I thought I had seen it all, but then I was meeting student leaders who were criticizing the government without fear. I wondered if they were not afraid of being arrested? That new experience allowed me to start questioning so many issues I had taken for granted. I started seeing and realizing that life in Zimbabwe was getting difficult and was no longer the same as it was in the 1980s. At the university, I could now start to see how the government was being accused of destroying the country, contrary to what I witnessed in the early 1980s. In my early years, I had been told that our government was one of the best because the country was still self-sufficient. How come at university I was now being told that the government had been wrong and corrupt since long back? The cost of living in the late 1990s started to soar, life was hard, and the social fabric of life I grew up knowing was being eroded.

I became very critical to the deterioration in our standards of living and started participating in university demonstrations against bad governance, privatization of university education among the many issues of our time as students. On a personal level, my life was getting difficult. The university at one stage was closed for six months after demonstrations, and that meant my time to complete the degree was also affected. My problems reached their zenith in my final year. University education had been privatized, and the government was no longer providing subsidized meals in halls of residence. That meant that it became increasingly difficult for me to afford the three meals a day I used to have when I started university in 1997. In my final year, I was offered residence at Mount Royal in Harare City Centre, and that place was mainly for medical students. I started my final year in March 2000, and during that time I could hardly afford to eat one meal a day. A plate of sadza (Zimbabwean staple food made out of corn meal) and stew which was the cheapest dish costing 6 Zimbabwean dollars. Within three years the cost of sadza and stew had skyrocketed, it was now 500 dollars. The inflation was caused by many factors in the politics and economics of Zimbabwe. During that time Zimbabwe was participating in a costly war in the Democratic Republic of Congo (DRC), and concurrently seizing white-owned farms among many other factors. That meant the Zimbabwean dollar which used to trade officially with the US dollar at about 1 US:16 Zimbabwean dollars when I started university, was no longer pegged at that level in the year 2000. In the year 2000, there was now a new language which was not there in 1997 like official rate and black-market rate for foreign currency. Life was deteriorating quickly in Zimbabwe, and one had to improvise to make ends meet.

For me to survive, I managed to forge an agreement with a second-year university Economics student who was a non-resident at the university seeking a place to stay. We agreed that the student would sublet space in my room in exchange for money. That was a private arrangement which was not allowed under the policy at the Mount Royal residence. I had to emphasize to the student to be discreet and to not expose the arrangement. Our deal was discovered. Mount Royal residence facility was not a big place; it was a residence where everybody knew each other, and the Warden who was responsible for it knew everyone in the dwelling. Therefore, it did not take long for our deal to be foiled.

I was called to the Warden's office and told that my tenancy had been withdrawn and was supposed to find alternative accommodation. I didn't take that lightly, and I tried every trick in the book to delay the inevitable, but the Warden could not entertain any of that. I continued to play hide and seek and slept in my bedroom, but it was not long until the Warden caught me. He told me to vacate the residence, and I went to his office in a tense mood and knocked on his door. He was not willing to entertain me and the next minute I heard him wailing, alleging that when he opened the door telling me to go away, I had pushed it towards him and injured his hand. He was in a mood to get rid of me for good, and he quickly bandaged himself telling me that he was going to report me to the Vice Chancellor that I assaulted him.

I was shocked by the turn of events, and while I was still in denial of being expelled from the residence, I now faced the prospect of being expelled from university for the false assault accusation. The Warden went and reported me to the Vice Chancellor that I had assaulted him. I couldn't say anything because it was his word against mine. I was taken aback by that new development, and I was at the mercy of university powers who were mostly against students during those days because of demonstrations that stopped the smooth flow of things at the campus. I feared the worst for my life and that was my final year. My parents were invited to meet the Vice-Chancellor regarding that issue; they traveled a three-hour journey from Mutare to Mount Pleasant (University location). My mother wept in the presence of the Vice Chancellor and asked him not to expel me from the university. The Vice-Chancellor was understanding, so he told my parents that I would no longer be dismissed, but I had to vacate Mount Royal residence. That was a major setback for me at the time and was caught up in conflicting feelings of luck and despair. I was lucky that the Vice Chancellor did not expel me but felt clueless on how to resolve my plight of homelessness.

I considered going to live with my sister, Netsai who was now married and living in Eastlea (low-density suburbs in the city of Harare) with three young daughters at the time. Eventually, I decided to find the courage and survive the harsh system and lifestyle that Zimbabwe was becoming. I went and talked to my young brother who was now an Accounts Clerk at A1 Taxi Association in Harare. He was now renting a place in Eastlea. I swallowed my pride and asked for favors from him, culturally the older brother is expected to look after everyone. In no time we were staying together, and I managed to finish my studies at the university, but my spirit had been hardened by experiencing the injustices of the country's system.

My first job after graduating was as a History and Religious Education teacher of students doing their Form three and four (3rd and 4th year of high school) at Chitora Secondary School in Mutare North. While at Chitora, the whole political, economic and social fabric of the country continued to spiral downward at a fast pace. I had always been fighting against injustice when I was a student at the university, and once again, I found myself caught up in politics as an activist for justice. As a result, I ran into trouble again and decided to run away from Zimbabwe, to seek sanctuary in England and claimed asylum in November 2008.

I was fortunate that I did not experience any problems with my application and was granted refugee status three months after claiming. The system was new to me. Fortunately, I had friends and family who were already in the United Kingdom to provide me with information whenever I needed it. I sought employment. I heard fond stories of Zimbabweans working as caregiver, and I thought to myself that should be the way for me as well. I secured my first job as a Care Assistant in a residential nursing home in July 2009. My experiences at that job took me back to the early 1980s period in Zimbabwe. One of my best friends at the nursing home was a man from Mozambique, and I began to ask myself many questions, I wondered why as a country we mistreated

Mozambicans. Here in England I was now getting most of my help from Antonio and began to realize that as Africans we are brothers. My world view was changing as well, and my new workplace was comprising of different citizens of the world that included Pakistan, India, Poland, Nigeria, Ghana, Mozambique, South Africa, and England. I had been offered sanctuary in England, and I was being treated with kindness and respect by the English who are a different race. When I was growing up in Mutare I didn't see the treatment I was now receiving here from the English being accorded to the Mozambicans. That made me wonder whether that was karma, maybe the problems we were experiencing as Zimbabweans were due to the way we used to treat others in need?

I considered my work as temporary while I was putting my feet on the ground and learning the new English system. In no time I identified social work as a vocation to pursue because I saw myself as having the potential to provide something unique and beneficial to my new community. I was willing to learn, and I started a journey in learning social work where I gained a variety of new vital skills. This new vocation transformed me and those around me. It transformed me in the sense that the ethos of social work complements my beliefs because social work is a vocation that promotes social change and development, social cohesion and the empowerment and liberation of people to enhance well-being. Principles of social justice, human rights, collective responsibility and respect for diversities are central to social work. In my daily work, I am guided by this definition of social work and this has enabled me to transform service users' lives. My role is to support different service user groups, and I have worked with refugee and asylum seekers who have been displaced from their countries of origin the same as me. I always work in the people's best interests and have represented my organization to write supporting letters to their claims which they take to the Tribunals for the Upper Tribunal Judges to decide. I have been to the Tribunals with people from different countries, and they always appreciate the work I do.

Displacement from my place of birth has resulted in me having empathy and compassion towards others. I continue to work in human services with a statutory duty of providing to others in need, and it is a duty that satisfies me, in the understanding that I continue to make a difference in people's lives.

Tendai Masiya

Tendai Masiya is a British citizen who resides in Stockport, Greater Manchester. He is a social worker and works for Birmingham City Council for their Children in Care Team. Tendai was born in Dangamvura, Mutare and is a second born in a family of three boys and two girls.

He was educated at the University of Zimbabwe and became influenced by student activism of his day. These views shaped Tendai, and due to this, he experienced political persecution in his first job after leaving the university at a secondary school in Mutare North. He migrated to England in 2008 to seek sanctuary and was recognized as a refugee by the British government.

Tendai pursued further education in the new host nation and is now a holder of a master's in social work qualification from Liverpool Hope University. Tendai follows Liverpool football club in his spare time.

tenayimasiya@yahoo.co.uk

LinkedIn-Tendai Masiya

Facebook- Tendai Masiya

Blossoming out of the Mud

By Roseanne de Beaudrap

In all my adult life so far, my motto has been to "Bloom where I'm planted." It has not always been easy to live by these words, as my husband and I have moved several times on our journey through life, and some parts of my childhood felt more like fertilizer than sunshine.

If you have ever tended a flower garden, you know that sometimes you need to add some fertilizer and it does not always smell like roses. That fertilizer that you add water to as you plant your seeds or as you set your bedding plants into that smelly mud, it nourishes your plant as it blooms forth to bring you joy and wonderment of life.

So, my first "Flower Garden of Life" began in Saskatchewan, Canada. I am the 6th born in a family of 5 girls and five boys. I am very adaptable with people of various age groups and personalities. When I was born, we were living in a small French village, and my Dad drove 16 miles to a farm to tend to the crops and animals. When I was three years old, we all moved to the farm. My Mom explained that it was because my Dad used the money she had saved for paying the taxes for "something else" and they lost the house. This move was a huge shift for us.

Both sets of grandparents and all my aunts, uncles and cousins stayed in the village area - the "French Catholic" area. We had crossed over into the other county - the "English Protestant" area.

My oldest brother and all my four sisters had been attending school in the French Village, and all classes were conducted in French. They had to adapt to the English spoken at the new school. We were all English immersed, that was for sure.

When I started school, I did not have a good grasp of the English language, and for a time I was labeled that "Dumb French Kid." Several experiences at the new school could be considered as "fertilizer mud," but that will be for a different story. My story shows how difficulties in life do not have to hold us back. People can choose to take different directions in life and bloom forth in love in spite of the negatives that they experience.

We were driven to school by bus. After completing our early morning chores, we were the first country school students on the bus route, and the last dropped off at the end of the school day. It was early evening when we arrived home to change; do our chores and then homework.

We were 12 miles south of town at the end of the road. The closest neighbour was 4 miles away, and if anyone wanted to phone us, they would call to that neighbour who would have to drive over and tell us the message, or we would have to drive back to their place to use their phone and call back. On a positive note, we had excuses for visits that way.

Our little farmhouse was only about 750 square feet - the kitchen and living room on the main floor with two and a half bedrooms upstairs. The largest room was divided in the middle with a curtain separating my two younger brothers' bed from the girls' side, and my parent's room with the little crib tucked into the corner. The open space at the top of the stairs was for my oldest brother's single bed.

There was no lovely bathroom in this house except in the winter a 5-gallon pail with a toilet lid over it in the small dirt basement was our luxury otherwise it was a frozen trip to the "Out-House."

When I went back three years ago and stood in that kitchen, I marveled at how we all fit into that small space. It is no wonder we spent most of our time outside.

Of course, with ten children there were always chores to be done inside and outside the house, and the seasonal work still kept us very busy. Our source of heat was the wood stove in the kitchen, a potbellied stove in the dirt basement to heat the kitchen floor, and the oil heater in the living room. On those early winter mornings, we got dressed under our blankets because the house was freezing. My eldest brother and sister were always the first ones up to light the stove with the dying embers of coal that would have been added to the wood before retiring the night before. No central heating, no phone, no indoor plumbing, so that meant we ran down to the well by the garden for our water. At least we had electricity for the pump at the well, which was quite a distance from the house. As a result, this made laundry day quite a chore as we hauled water in and filled the wringer washer then hauled all the dirty water out. After the laundry was done came hauling in more water for bath time.

It is no wonder we only had baths once a week and, in the summer, I remember Mom washing our little feet before bedtime because we had been out barefoot all day.

We had the physiological needs of water, food, and warmth on Maslow's Hierarchy of needs. It was not quite in the same way as the rest of the community who had telephones, modern plumbing, and heating systems but I guess one could say we were living semi "off grid" since we did have electricity for our lights and for running the pump at the well.

In the next level of Maslow's hierarchy of needs are safety and security – for us that was where things started to fall apart a bit. Though we had the safety and security of a warm, cozy house, we shared it with several mice, and we could hear them scratching in the walls. Their evidence was in the kitchen cookbook pages they nibbled at. We laughed at that - the best recipes had been chewed up. We developed a dark humour as a coping mechanism to shed some light on our dark days. Mom helped us to see the twisted funny side of our circumstances. I only appreciated her strength after I became a mother myself.

It was the mental safety where I presumed there were gaps. My Dad suffered from mental health issues. The stress of the Spring planting and the Fall harvesting were the most difficult times for him, which also affected us. I was told of 4 different times he was admitted to the Saskatchewan Mental Hospital. The first time was when I was only a few months old, the 2nd when I was 3, when I was 7, and when I was nine years old. That 2nd visit was initiated because Mom had taken my sister to the Doctor to tend to a severe gash on her head. The Doctor asked Mom how that had happened. She was afraid of the consequences of revealing the truth, so she said my sister had tripped and fallen against the table.

The Doctor remarked, "No child gets hurt this badly by tripping. Tell me the Truth!"

There was no other way but tell the truth, and the police were sent to deal with Dad who was then taken to the Mental Hospital. After a few months-stay, he was sent back home with medications.

However, since he did not believe that he needed those pills, the tumultuous life continued for us as before.

Usually, if a "disaster" had happened for my Dad, someone else was to blame so we all, Mom and us kids, got to be punished. It was dramatic!

We, the children, would all be lined up to get the strap, which was the leather strap from the horse harness, folded in two for double effect. Most times it was used on our bottoms, leaving welts on thighs for a few days, and other times the strapping was on our hands.

During the summer when I was 6 and shortly before one of the hand-strapping events, I accidentally scalded my wrist on the stove as I was climbing down off my perch.

I had been combing my hair and looking into the mirror by the sink. When I was scooting down, I leaned on the stove for support not knowing it was still hot from the morning fire, so the subsequent hand strapping on both extended little hands broke open the scab, which had just started healing.

I honestly do not recall the lesson we all had to learn that day, but the strapping happened, and the scar on my right wrist remains.

Later that Fall my younger brother died. I can still hear my Mom's ragged sobs echoing in the house. At the time I was told that the cause of his death was measles spots that were in his lungs.

Mom told me that the house was too cold so instead of the spots coming out onto his skin they stayed in the lungs causing terrible severe pneumonia. The medicines of the day were not effective enough to heal him.

I remember the crib being brought down to the living room and placed next to the furnace. I remember Mom in her pink housecoat as she cuddled him. It was not until I was in my 40's that one of my sisters told me the rest of the story.

An old claw foot tub was in our front yard close to the west flower bed. On hot summer days, we would have fun splashing about. However, on that chilly Fall day, a laundry day, it was not fun. My sister, who would have been 11 years old, was hanging clothes on the clothesline… and my younger brother, 2&1/2 years old, was digging in the flower bed perhaps taking some water from that tub from the recent rain to water those flowers that he was "planting and tending" for Mom. Unfortunately, Dad was in one of his rages and on his way back from the barn he saw my little brother digging in the flower bed with his small play shovel. Whatever it was that had already enraged him, his anger was worsened when he saw him digging in the muddy dirt, apparently ruining the flower bed, which was already destroyed by the frost - nothing was growing in it.

Regardless of that, Dad picked up my brother and pushed him face down into the tub with that cold water.

My sister looked on in horror and knew better than to yell "Stop!" as that would have made things worse. Whenever Dad was told to stop, he would prolong the torture because no one was going to tell him what to do.

She ran to the house, and when she reached the door, she turned to look back and saw our little brother's wet body with a blue face being held up by Dad. I believe that Mom had been told that our brother had fallen into the tub accidentally. After a night in the crib by the furnace, he was taken 45 miles away to the hospital while we were at school. My sister recalled to me how heartbroken she was that she had not had a chance to say goodbye. She was informed that she could see him at the hospital later but her intuition at the time knew she would never see him again.

At his funeral, I remember wanting to kiss his sweet little face to wake him up. I was told that he would wake up in heaven and play with Jesus. Later at the house, I could hear those anguished sobs shaking the walls, coming from my parent's bedroom while all of us children were comforting each other in the living room. I remember Dad coming down the stairs and looking into the room, at us. What my sister told me, but I do not remember the details, that he looked directly at my sister who had witnessed this horror and said he was sorry; before walking out of the house. I cannot even imagine what he must have been going through on so many levels. After many years I forgave him. I do not know, nor do I want to know, the monsters that lurked in his mind.

At times pieces of my past childhood puzzle float in my daydream as I remember snippets of my younger, formative years. For example, one snippet was hiding in the little coat closet by the kitchen door. It was a cupboard with hooks for coats but no door on it. I wanted to hit my Dad with the broom, but what good would that have done? I wanted to hit him to make him stop! He had a rifle in one hand and reaching for the bullets that my Mother was trying to keep away from him. My Father's reach was longer than hers, so I do not know how she managed this. I do remember her yelling.

"You don't want to do this!"

You see he was going to end it all for us.

The reality that Dad might act on his word is something my eldest sister feared daily; terrified that she would come home from school and find us all shot dead. Those two rifles were hung above the kitchen door, and I am grateful the bullets were stored away in the cupboard by the sink. Their purpose was for the protection of unexpected intruders during the night, human or animal.

My eldest sister lived with this daily visceral fear because from the age of 8 to 15, our Father sexually abused her, and he had threatened her that if she were to tell he would kill us all. Therefore, seeing him holding the rifle while in such rage would undoubtedly cement that as a REAL truth.

I do not know for a fact how Dad's unwanted attentions affected my other sisters or whether it ever happened to any others, as I have not discussed details with them. Even though Dad is now gone, it is uncomfortable to bring up the past.

I came to know that there was such a thing as "non-physical" sexual abuse when I was 12 years old. It was winter, and I was standing with my back to the stove warming myself when Dad came into the house. Before taking off his coat, he stood there staring at me and said, "Your chest is almost as big as your Mother's."

It made me feel very intimidated.

I said, "Don't look at me like that."

"I can do anything I want to you! You're my daughter!" he replied. I instantly felt powerless, disgusted, dirty, ashamed, vulnerable, horrified and full of fear. That was stored deep within my psyche and cellular memory - things like that seep out of storage when you least expect it.

During that beautiful first intimate time with my husband, all of those memories came flooding back. I cried on end.

My gentle husband held me and kissed my tears away. I was his now. He loved and cherished me and would always protect me. I found safety and security in his loving heart - a safe harbor in his embrace.

The physical, sexual molestation that happened to me occurred with another family member as well as with a member of my church community. The earliest time I remember was from the age of about four years old and the last memory I have of it was when I was about 11 years old. It boggles my mind how no one "noticed" anything. When children are being abused, their behavior changes - I suppose when you are in a house of trauma the little things go un-noticed as the primary objective is merely to survive.

Where was the Community, the school, the church or the elders? The obvious marks of physical abuse were visible, yet it was a culture of "don't get involved"; so, there was never an investigation.

These experiences have bothered me for years and affected the way I felt about myself causing quite a lot of self-esteem issues resulting in relationship problems.

It was only when I started forgiving those who had hurt me that I forgave myself and then I began to heal. I forgave myself for feeling shame that I had in any way made them believe they could do this to me. I have learned that many victims feel shame and yet we are not the perpetrators.

Of course, that was a false belief. My child's brain was trying to make sense of things. I am sure there were many more false beliefs connected to how powerless, hurt, confused, fearful, and disgusted I was feeling about these males who were my family and in my "safe" church community. They were the males that I looked up to and feared at the same time. As an adult, I forgave them and began to heal. They never asked ME for forgiveness … I did that for my own peace.

It took several years of counseling, praying, weeping, guided meditations, talking with my friends and my sisters, battling a "quiet, mild depression," doing Emotional Freedom Technique, receiving Reiki sessions, and through all of this, my belief in God's love to heal. I believed that God is in my heart and their hearts as well and that God loves us ALL unconditionally, that enabled me to let go. I understood they had not had an ideal childhood either and that affected their behavior.

It was healing through the mud of my past, so I can bloom where I am planted and help others on their "healing journey."

I began my path to healing in my 20's. I experienced a lot of anger and self-doubt. I wrote many letters that I never mailed but that helped me get it out of my system - out of my cells, my DNA, where all THAT had been stuffed. I had shown one of my sisters just one of the letters I wrote to Dad, and she said this would not make any difference as he would never take any responsibility for what he had done.

She had gone to him and asked WHY he had done ALL this to us. His answer was simply, "I only wanted you kids, to love me." Her response had been, "How could we love you when we were in so much FEAR of you!?"

For years I have served clients as a practitioner of many body-mind-spirit healing techniques; including EFT (tapping), Crystal Bowl Meditations and Reiki, always searching for something that would help me and benefit my clients as well. Even with all this, there was still something missing in my quest for inner peace around my past and finding the confidence in myself to change my future; I feel fortunate to have found another healing modality, that has had a profound impact on my life. I have become a certified MAP Coach (MAP stands for Manifesting All Possibilities) which is a gentle way to release the niggling, bothersome memories that reared their presence in my daytime dreams and in some night time ones as well. It worked so well for me that I decided to delve right in and study this so that I could help others.

I am so grateful and happy that I now have a way to help my clients heal from this type of abuse and memories that may be haunting them, possibly causing them to have low self-esteem as I have had for far too long. I now offer MAP sessions. It is a gentle yet powerful way to help neutralize and release memories never to be triggered by them again. I simply command the subconscious, with permission from my client, to tag and treat all parts of the memory that need healing. With the sessions that I have already done with my clients, they have reported not being triggered by the issues we worked on. Sometimes another layer of something else comes up to be released, and we work on whatever arises. Also, I am encouraged that several of my clients have said that some chronic physical pain had disappeared since the previous session - this is proof to me that when we experience trauma, this event gets imprinted into our cells, into our DNA, into our physical body, and we aren't even aware of it. Cellular memory holds "issues in our tissues" – so, even though my client and I had not even verbally addressed the physical issue - it is just released gently as a result of the memory being released during the session.

I am not only a Coach; I also love BEING Coached by another MAP practitioner. Now that I have had some of these gentle releases with MAP, I feel so much more grounded, more self-confident and focused. I wish the same for others who are suffering from emotional traumas. They deserve freedom and joy in their lives. They can reach out to me or anyone else that has been trained as a MAP coach and start a new chapter in their lives.

It is crucial for me to tell others who struggle with various mental health issues, that if I can do it, they can do it.

Take your past "fertilizer" and use it as your energy and nourishment to grow…grow stronger and more radiant … keep improving on your healing journey.

Roseanne de Beaudrap

Roseanne de Beaudrap has worn many professional hats and most recently the hat of being a Wholistic Registered Massage Therapist for the past 16 years. She specializes in treatments for women and children. When looking for the best way to help her clients, Roseanne treats each individuals' mind, body and spirit as a whole. She provides some holistic modalities that are often custom blended for her clients' benefit. She believes we do not get sick all at once; it happens slowly over time. We create an environment where discomfort, disease, and sickness can thrive.

Roseanne shares a story of forgiveness from the abusive childhood she sprouted from and intends to give hope to her readers. She believes forgiveness is a gift of inner peace we give to ourselves and the positive ripples they create are beneficial to all. In this little way, we can all bloom where we are planted.

To connect with Roseanne:

www.sacredwinds.ca

sacredwindshealing@gmail.com

Forever in My Heart

By Janet Hativagone Maponga

When I walked into my sister Hilda's hospital room, it was packed as usual with family and friends who came to see her. Although the number of patients' visitors was restricted to only six at a time, the evening visiting hours always attracted more people as it was more convenient for them to pass through the hospital after work. This made my sister tired, and for the most part, she just closed her eyes and listened to them as they chit chatted until they left. While she appreciated the visitors, I believe sometimes it overwhelmed her. The efforts by the nursing staff and immediate family to stagger the visitors' visiting times went unheeded. People still came and left at their convenience.

After greeting everyone, about thirteen people in the room at that time, I went and sat on the bed next to her. There were no empty chairs obviously, but I still preferred to sit on her bed as close to her as possible. I would hold her hand and talk to her quietly, encouraging her to open her eyes. She always did, a faint smile on her face. It was like our secret but most of all I didn't want her to feel alone in a room full of people. I also wanted her to feel loved and cared for, and I believe she did.

Soft music played in the background. It was music by my sister's favorite singer Tuku. I remember how she used to follow Tuku around and hardly missed his concerts when he performed in the city. At home, she sang along to his music. She didn't have the voice. She was not talented that way, but that didn't stop her.

She had been in the hospital for close to a month, and the prognosis was not good. After the doctor had done his ward rounds, the multidisciplinary team recommended hospice for end of care.

My sister was in a lot of pain and was medicated which often led her to sleep a lot. When she was awake, she tried hard not to show it. She had always been that person, strong, a fighter so full of energy until she was diagnosed with pancreatic cancer two years before her passing. It was stage four then, and there wasn't much they could do for her. It was a waiting game, excruciating for both her and us. But deep down I still hoped for a miracle; I hoped the doctors were wrong, that she would somehow recover. I was not ready for the end that seemed so near. It terrified me.

I kept my eyes on her and wondered what was going on in her head. What was it that she was thinking about all this time? Was she afraid of death? That much I didn't know, but one of her fears was leaving her two young girls behind. She had tried to bargain with God so many times. She didn't know what would happen to them when she was gone. Unfortunately, instead of getting better she only grew worse, weaker every day. The sickness continued to rob her of her ability to be a mother to the girls, or wife, or sister. It robbed her of her happiness, and her independence to lead a normal life. It was torture, to watch her go through this.

I made sure I was by her side all the way right to the end. I was constant. She urged me several times to have a life, but I told her I had a life. She was my life; this was my life. I couldn't live any other life. It felt wrong and selfish for me to be anywhere else doing whatever else. For as long as she needed me, I was going to be there for her. I wanted to help my sister until she got better. I had graduated from high school and was supposed to start my secretarial course at one of the local colleges. I decided to put it on hold, but I never told her. The course would always be there, and I could do it any time, and I knew she wouldn't.

When the doctor discharged her, the nurses prepared her to leave the hospital. The palliative nurses would come to the house to check on her, but it was her husband and me who would do most of the bedside care; bathing her, repositioning her, and feeding her. She wasn't eating much, just a teaspoonful of soup or yogurt or just water to keep her mouth from getting too dry. Since her condition was deteriorating fast, my eldest brother Ted wanted her in his house. It was one of her end-of-life wishes not to die in the hospital but at home and he was honoring it. The husband was okay with the decision since he didn't want their twin 9-year-old girls to see their mother suffering that much. We had always been a close-knit family since the passing of our parents and Ted had done all he could to keep the family together.

During the early hours of the following Saturday, we watched her as she slowly slipped into death with all her siblings and husband at her bedside. Despite all the suffering she had gone through, and the fact that she was not in pain anymore, her passing was not easy to accept.

I loved my sister. I just wanted her back, whole not sick. We were as close as any sisters could be; this was yet another death in the family. It should have been easier for me to handle because I had seen her go through this painful journey, but it wasn't. Instead, I started thinking more about my mother, how she had died. Was it cancer as well? Dad passed on when I was two, but with mom, I was about eight years old. I did remember her somehow, and the family pictures did help a lot. I sometimes wondered how my life or my sister's and other siblings' lives would be like if she had lived?

What terrified me more was the fact that I was about the same age as my nieces when my mom died. Now, these two girls were being forced to go through life without their mother too at about the same age. Was this some kind of pattern? Did I need to get checked for cancer also? Would it happen to me when I marry and have children? When death takes your mother, it steals the word MOM forever from your vocabulary. I had no one to call mom, and my sister's children had no one to call mom too. It terrified me.

What would become of their life? We had been blessed to have a brother who was so caring and had put his life on hold, to take care of me and my other siblings when our parents passed on. My sister's husband Simba was still young, and the chances were that he would remarry. Knowing someone would take over my sister's place as their mother was a hard pill to swallow. I was really struggling. What made it more painful was the fact that no one in the family ever talked about mom, not her illness or what exactly killed her. I knew she was sick for a while then went to live with her sister in the village until she passed on. Why the village? I had so many questions that I never asked. No one volunteered any information either.

I then decided I was going to be a nurse. I thought part of me would be connected to my sister that way, reminding me of how I took care of her. I don't know what good that was supposed to do me, but it was my one wish, and I obsessed over it. It felt good knowing that I had given her my all although she still died. At least I didn't feel guilty on that part.

However, it was very competitive to get into the nursing schools in Zimbabwe then, and since I couldn't get into one, I had no choice but to shelf my dream career and settled for the next thing, which was a being secretary.

I met my husband at work. We got married and had three children. He was a good man, a good father to the children but I realized that deep down I was unhappy. From the outside, I didn't have any reason to be unhappy. My marriage was as good as it could be. We had our issues just like any other marriage but nothing to write home about. I appreciated my husband, but I just couldn't share with him my fears and thoughts. I couldn't share with anyone what I was going through.

Ten years later we migrated to the United Kingdom. I still struggled with the loss of my sister, and the mother I never really got to know. The void that her death left continued to torment me. It was something I never talked to anyone about. No one knew, but I agonized over it. My husband encouraged me to go to nursing school. He knew about my passion for being a nurse. I was hesitant at first. Now that I had the opportunity for my dream career, I didn't know if being in the hospital would do me any good as I was sure it would bring back memories of my sister since she was in the hospital a lot after her cancer diagnosis. Hospitals have a terrible vibe sometimes. I really had no good reason not to do it, my kids were not young anymore, and it was a second opportunity in life.

Even though I was out of school for about twenty years, I managed to get into nursing school. The three years in nursing school were not a bed of roses, but I managed to pass and got a job at a hospital. If anything, I was comfortable helping the sick people. It was déjà vu.

During my second week after orientation, I admitted a thirty-three-year-old female who had pancreatic cancer. Like my sister, she was jaundiced too, and the prognosis was not good. Lila, reminded me so much of my sister who will always be thirty-three years old, the age she was when she died. Lila's family consisted of two older sisters, the mom, nieces, and nephews who came often to see her in the hospital. The mother and one of the sisters were always in the room with her. She was never left alone, not even for a second. They had lots of flowers from well-wishers. That's one thing my sister never wanted. She, for some reason, associated the flowers with death when she was sick. We never had any in her room just some get well cards. She didn't mind those. They had lots of family pictures too and some on the ceiling, so she would see them when she lay on her back instead of the plain white ceiling. There was something about the atmosphere in the room; it was different. It was not sadness. When I went in to take care of Lila, I felt both sad and joyful; sad that she was sick, and the prognosis was not good but joyful because the family was there for her and had accepted the situation. For her they had made the room homely. Lila was my patient for the three weeks she was in the hospital. I got to know the family well

One day on my way home I met the mother in the parking lot as I was heading to my car. We started chatting. I asked how she was holding up. She told me she was doing okay and all she wanted was for her daughter to know that she is loved and that she is not alone. She said Lila had a good life until the disease took over, and that if she passed on, she believed she was going to a better place. She told me they had accepted her fate and thanked God every day for the time they had with her. This was something different for me; it didn't make sense. What was there to accept? It was food for thought though.

When Lila passed on a week later, the family invited the ward staff to her funeral. I had grown attached to the family, so I decided to go with another staff member. At the funeral, I realized that the mother did not shed a tear but when her siblings cried, I cried with them, but it was more for my mother and sister than for Lila.

My crying so hard for a patient I had only known for a short time did not go unnoticed. Lila's mother could somehow tell that I was crying for more than Lila. When she asked me what was going on, I did open up to her and told her about my struggle with my mom and sister's death. She explained to me that she had lost her husband to cancer too. She believed in celebrating her beloved's lives instead of moaning.

"Each day I spend with my family is a gift and I don't take it for granted. I don't think about why it happened, or why my daughter or husband had to die. I believe we are all here for a reason, a purpose. Our time will come too but it is important for the loved ones to do all they can to take care of their sick, so they don't feel guilty when they are finally gone. While it is difficult to accept their demise, it is just as hard to watch them go through so much pain. Always celebrate their lives and thank God for the time you had them."

She told me to think seriously about what she had said, and I did. When I told her, I had chosen this career for my sister; she told me that I should always remember where I got the training from, and that should motivate me to be the nurse that would make my sister proud of me.

I admired this family's acceptance of the situation and that they had kept going through the hard times hard as it was. I had learned a thing or two from them.

That was my turning point. My sister and mother had lived their lives, and I believed they were at peace wherever they were. I thought they wanted me to be happy too. From that moment, I decided I would be celebrating their lives. When I got home, I went into my bedroom, locked myself in and cried. I cried so hard for both my mom and sister. I could not hold back the tears. When I was done with crying which I told myself was the last time, I felt like a heavy load had been lifted off my shoulders. I decided to start living a life that would make them proud of me.

I sat my two girls down one evening before bedtime and brought out some family photos that I had always kept hidden. They were surprised because they knew I never wanted to talk about my sister or their grandmother. Honestly, pleasure shone in their eyes, and it brought me so much joy. My mom was their grandmother and my sister their aunt.

They didn't have to be a secret anymore. Although I didn't have much to say about my mom, except she was a beautiful, strong woman, I had lots to say about my sister whom I adored so much.

I had been stuck in this personality for too long, and it was time for me to get my life back. It was not going to happen overnight, but I had started, and that was the best part. Opening up to my husband and children was an excellent way to start.

In the process, I realized that you could never know peace until you learn to let go of the hurt that lives inside you. Life is too short and why not enjoy it with the loved ones in case something happens they will have good things to think about and share with their families. Although I tried to hide it, I believe my family to an extent knew how unhappy I was. They just didn't know why exactly, or how to help me since I didn't share with them my internal struggles. I also decided that the next time I went back home to Zimbabwe, I would ask lots of questions about that woman I call mom, and whom I knew only for the first eight years of my life. She was and will always be my mom, but I still could get to know more about her. All I needed to do was ask. I believe the two of them are together somewhere with dad too watching over me, this time smiling.

Janet Hativagone Maponga

Janet Hativagone Maponga is a mother of three. She was born and raised in Harare, Zimbabwe. She is a well determined and vigorous person and yet pleasantly quiet. She encourages fighting for what your desires are and believes in doing so through God the Almighty who makes everything possible.

She received BSc. Honors degree in Nursing from the University of Cambridge in the United Kingdom where she resides. On completion, she joined one of the University hospitals. Janet has extensive experience in various healthcare sectors. Before studying for nursing, she worked as a caregiver/support worker for 14 years.

Due to busy work, she hardly gets time to spare for other things. However, her love for learning and success motivates her to utilize her limited time focuses on improving her skills and knowledge to succeed in today's society.

She enjoys reading fictional science stories which she finds more appealing to her imagination. She enjoys spending time with her husband and an adorable daughter.

To connect with Janet:

maponjane@ymail.com

https://www.facebook.com/rprudence

Desires Stay True

By Adeola Olayemi

Growing as a child, I was obsessed with serving humanity, helping the needy, devoting all my energy to those who were helpless. Though as a profession I wanted to be an engineer and nothing else, I dreamt of being a philanthropist. I wanted to be the next Ben Carson of this generation - to have a think-big story - I knew breaking out of my shyness would make me a better adult. At some point in my teenagehood, I found it difficult to express my opinion about certain issues, even to my friends. Often I would acquire knowledge from watching a movie or reading a novel, but I still found it difficult to share the new experience with friends. Expressing my opinion about anything was a great challenge for me. I felt no one would agree or accept my views and that I was not good enough. I was afraid of criticism. Today I know better. I have come to realize I am entitled to my happiness, opinion, peace of mind and I have a voice.

It sounds like a missed opportunity when I say that I never gained admission into the University to study my dream course, civil engineering. Let alone to go in the field to deliver skilled jobs by creating good roads. However, I had an opportunity to walk on a path that I am now grateful I chose.

Like every child, I had people I looked up to, several of which were total strangers - they were people I could do anything to spend an hour with, to know how they paved through the world to achieve their goals. One of these persons was Julius Berger, the world-renowned construction magnate whose construction company – Julius Berger – built most of our bridges and many Nigerian edifices.

My Dad works for a civil engineering company as an automobile engineer. I usually followed him to the office on weekends, and I imagined myself in those boots, helmet, and suits. I loved the engineering profession because I felt that society would be incomplete without them. One of the places we passed through on our way to my Dad's office was the Third Mainland Bridge, which was constructed in 1990 and up to date, happens to be the second longest bridge in Africa. Whenever we crossed the bridge, I was always amazed by the beautiful architectural design of the bridge, let alone the brilliance of the engineers who were involved in the design and construction.

My country was known for its bad roads, and I knew to become a civil engineer was one way to solving that problem and the woes of vehicle owners. Apart from dreaming of having become the first female civil engineer to construct a proper road back then, I wanted to drive my new car for a long distance without worrying about hitting stones, bumps, and potholes. My Dad would always smile at me when I told him about my dream to become the next Julius Berger, but my Mom just knew within her that I was never supposed to be an engineer – time would tell what I would become.

Apart from having dreams of becoming a civil engineer, I also wanted to be known for my good deeds - to have compassion for others. I wanted to do all I could to see a world free of sicknesses, unnecessary deaths, and of course a life filled with happiness. I wanted a future where I could impact people's lives. I wanted to be a nurse.

Days rolled in and out and the time to make a choice came. I wrote my first examination to get admitted into the civil engineering curriculum at a technology school. I was not admitted to the curriculum because I failed my exam. I was heartbroken, devastated and ashamed of my failure. I cried, but I was not ready to give up either. Holding on to my dreams consoled me. I kept telling myself that one day I would be a civil engineer. My mom was my guardian angel. She told me to drop chasing the wrong dreams. She went on to say that civil engineering was a masculine profession, and I was far too emotional to solve technical problems in road construction, for example building bridges. Sometimes our failures are one way of knowing that we may not be on the right path - I failed my civil engineering entry examinations twice. My mom felt that I was a very sensitive and compassionate person. She advised me to choose to go to nursing school, but it did not make sense then. However, I gave nursing a thought, and I fell in love with it. I do not know what my mother had seen in me, but in hindsight, it makes sense now.

The journey into nursing started from knowing that hundreds of families depended on me as a professional. When a patient dies in my hands, several others' dreams die alongside them. The relatives feel hopeless, sad, and heartbroken and they wish I could bring their loved ones back to life - but alas the person is gone. Each day in the ward gives me a new definition of life, relationships, love, and family. I have become stronger and more intelligent and aware of what matters the most. I can now control my emotions. I have learned to be a good listener and to be there for my patients' families.

Just like writing, storytelling is essential; it makes the story real to the readers, so does nursing. I have learned to use the art of storytelling in the hospital wards. I tell my patients about other patients whom I have seen go through the same pain as them (respecting the confidentiality of course) and how they sailed through. When telling the stories, I sympathize and empathize with them. I tell them I am human and whatever they are going through can happen to anyone including me, but all that matters is doing the right thing by staying in the hospital bed, correctly taking their medication and listening to good medical counsel.

The truth about nursing is that every day is not always the best day. I do not leave work happy every day, but I try to leave work like a victor. It simply means, even when I lose a patient to the cold hands of death, I am convinced that I would have given the patient care, love to allow for a painless and peaceful passage.

The first time I built a personal connection with my patient was during my first year in nursing school. I will call her Rose for privacy. Rose was a pink warrior, and she was in her last stage of breast cancer. All we had to do was give her palliative care. That was the first time I saw an adult groan in pain because of cancer. I had heard stories and read about it in the past, but never experienced watching someone go through it. That one experience taught me so many life lessons. It taught me to hold on to family, to God, and my faith.

Rose encouraged me when I was caring for her. She believed one day I was going to be a good nurse and she thought I was a good Christian. For the short time I spent caring for Rose, we managed to forge a mother-daughter relationship. She talked to me like the daughter she wished she had. I did my best to take good care of her, and I always prayed for her. I wished I had given her more good memories back then, but I did not know better, I was just a new student nurse. I was too worried about the prospect of losing her. I was despondent and did not know what to do.

I was heartbroken to hear that she had finally succumbed to her illness one Friday evening. I believe Rose died a victor though I just wished she had lived one more day. Even though we all knew life was nearing the end, it was difficult to accept.

Rose would have liked making videos of herself on the hospital bed or record her favorite songs or taking selfies of her and me. If I could, I would have done it for her, but I was still a new nurse, and I was not sure if it was appropriate.

I think of Rose every day that passes by, and every October I create an event to raise awareness for breast cancer because of her. Rose and I only knew each other for two weeks before she passed away. She taught me the greatest lesson of all times. The impact she made in my life will stay with me for the rest of my life. Even in her last moments, she became my teacher.

I have many more stories I can share about my interaction with patients. Overall, my journey from being a student nurse to becoming a nurse has been fulfilling. As a result of my profession, I have been totally transformed to become a very selfless person and offer patients unconditional support. Today I can comfortably make personal connections with people without doubting myself. Through nursing, I have gained the ability to be able to communicate with patients and allowing them to feel comfortable telling me about their health challenges without reservation. I have become an excellent sounding board for many, and the patients appreciate it. Because of my good listening skills, patients end up sharing stories about their siblings, children, and spouses. They are encouraged by my listening as they share their life lessons and sources of wisdom. Today I can say nursing has given me the skills to bring some normalcy under challenging circumstances. Being a nurse makes me feel like a victor, but I know that God is in control and I am only his instrument.

My transformation did not only end at being the person I just described. I have also become a nurse who is an advocate for empowering other nurses, and I communicate my message through writing articles. The way I tell stories to my patients is the same way I tell stories in my articles. Recently, I joined a nursing organization that is focused on empowering nurses in Nigeria and Africa at large. In my messages, I also bring awareness regarding the profession because sometimes I feel like the public does not give it enough credit. In all of my articles, I share good work practices so that other nurses learn how to become better in their vocation and to be empowered beyond it. I show them how to stand high without the fear of being insulted because of what people think of them. Some of my followers on social media tell me how I am changing their impression on nursing and how I have changed their opinions about who they are as nurses. I am often humbled when I read or hear words like *"I am glad I can change a person's perspective of nursing because of my act."*

In my articles, I am also writing health tips and general information regarding women's health and the power of faith. I encourage them to take preventative measure towards their health. Through sharing all this information on social media, in articles and books, I have managed to empower many women beyond just nurses. I have created a way for other women to reach out for help and advice regarding their health.

I am thankful for my profession because it has truly transformed my life. I have become a person who brings inspiration, smiles and hope to others, this has been quite a journey, and today I can say, I am living a fulfilling life serving humanity.

Olayemi Adeola

Olayemi Adeola is a professional nurse, who focuses on coaching young ladies' health wise. She is a passionate teen coach and dedicates her time to write on healthy living tips for teenagers. She is the founder of the Nurse Olayemi Adeola platform, a platform dedicated to teaching young ladies how to stay healthy in today's world. She is a volunteer at Mentally Aware Nigeria Initiative and is an advocate for mental health.

She is the author of Mental Health, a book that explains how best to stay mentally healthy. Olayemi is a young lady who is creative and passionate about her nursing career; she is a board executive at the Fellow Nurses Africa organization.

Connect with Adeola:

Facebook: Olayemi Mary Adeola

Twitter: Iam_theola

Instagram: @ademartiy

Holding on to What's Precious

By Chido Kusena

The word of God in the book of *Ephesians 6:1-3* reads, "Children obey your parents in the Lord, for this is right. **Honour your father and mother**...which is the first commandment with a promise...Ephesians goes on to say, "that it may go well with you and that you may live long in the land."

Exodus 20:12, "Honour **your father and your mother**, that your days may be long upon the land which the Lord your God is giving you." All these verses about loving and honouring our parents did not specify any conditions as to when to love our parents. So, whether good or bad, present or absent, loving or unloving, kind or cruel, faithful or unfaithful just love and honour them.

A statement that kept me in check was from my mother when she said to me one morning," Chido *nyangwe Baba vako vakatanga kupenga vachifamba vasina kupfeka* (if your Father was insane and walking around naked) it does not change the fact that he is your Dad, in fact, you should be the first one to go and cover him."

All this made sense to me on the 21st of April 2016 when we laid Daddy to rest.

Growing up I knew that all we had was Mum at home. She was responsible for everything including school expenses, clothing and food for us. Dad worked in another city far from home, and we would see him only when he came home on public holidays until he stopped coming home entirely. I remember one time when he came home on Heroes' Day (Public holiday to honor the Heroes who fought for the independence of Zimbabwe), he made us watch the Heroes day parade on television, and he started telling us about his personal experience during the war before Zimbabwe became an independent country in 1980. I was not enjoying his company; there was no bond at all between my father and me. I was feeling very sad and resentful towards him for not always being present in our lives.

Looking back, when I was about eight years old I remember going shopping with Mum and Dad and my late younger sister. It was fun, and we would get lovely clothes and just enjoyed spending time with both parents. During that time, my Dad used to come and visit us frequently, but by the time I was 15 years old those days were over, he rarely visited us.

I have a couple of memories I would like to share as I reflect on the frequency of his visits. I was about 15 years old when dad came home to visit and brought me a green costume. I did not like it because green was not my favorite color. However, I did not dwell too much on my feelings about the green costume. I figured it was the thought that counted. By then, I was beginning to have resentment towards him because he was coming home to visit us less frequent than he used to visit us in the past.

A few more years down that line, I had just finished taking national examinations in high school, a requirement for every 4th-year student in High school to fulfill before they graduate. In order to pass, you had to have five classes with a grade of at least a "C." Once you pass those national examinations, it was a passage to get into other opportunities to further your education. My Dad came home at that time with a wristwatch that he gave to me as a gift to congratulate me for completing my High school education. He was already convinced I would pass with flying colors, but I was not convinced. His belief in me was a clear sign of his love and trust towards me. My Dad believed in me even from a distance.

My dad was right. I passed my tests with flying colors and continued to go to "A" level. Zimbabwe's education system mimics the British system. One is required to complete six years of high school education before going to university. The first four years of high school earns you an "Ordinary Level" certificate. Depending on the grades one can go on to pursue the "Advanced Level" (2 additional years of high school) and if they pass they have a chance to go to the university. I did very well on my "Ordinary Level" tests, and I was fortunate to continue to pursue my "Advanced Level" (A Level) education at a boarding school.

At the boarding school, I shared a room with my longtime friend from childhood who was also doing "A" level. One day I shared a story which involved my dad, and my roommate was surprised. She commented that I had never talked about my dad in all the years she had known me. She just assumed he was dead. That was a moment when I realized I had grown distant from my dad.

I completed my "A" Level with flying colors, and I was about to go to the University in the same town my dad worked in as long as I could remember. By then, my resentment and anger towards my Dad was now very profound, and no one could tell me otherwise. Not even my Mum's[2] words at that time could make me feel different about him. My hatred towards him was because I questioned his lack of responsibility in my life as a father emotionally, financially, socially and spiritually.

My mother asked me to call my Dad and tell him that I had been enrolled at the university in the same town he was working. It was a struggle for me to do it, but I could never say no to my mother, so l had to do it. On the day that l called Dad he could not recognize my voice, so I simply hung up the phone and cried. I felt betrayed! If he was a loving father, he should have recognized my voice. Eventually, my brother intervened, and he called him to inform him the reason for my call.

I managed to get a place to rent out, and I started my university studies well without involving my Dad in the whole process. After several weeks I got in touch with my Dad just out of respect for my Mum's sake since she had requested me to do so. It was on a Sunday after church when we spoke on the phone, and we decided to meet. He took me downtown to the market place and showed me the area to get cheap fresh vegetables and uptown where he showed me beautiful suburbs. Along the way, he told me a bit of the history about the places. We passed through a hotel, and he joked that one day when you have a special someone, he would take you there for dinner. He also asked me where l was attending church and went on to say, "I don't think that your mother will like that very much if she hears that you are not going to the church, she raised you in." His comment surprised me. That showed me that he still had his family's values at heart. Only he knew why he was absent from the family for so long but clearly; he was aware of our existence and our beliefs.

That whole-time l had been burning to ask him why he had left us, but l could not do it. He later took me home where l was staying at the time, and he commented that if l had told him earlier, he could have helped me find a cheaper place to rent. That whole episode at the time did not make sense to me because l had a burning question in my heart, and I had no idea how he would have reacted if l had asked. Besides, in our culture it is considered disrespectful to question your parents' action or behavior, so l was caught up in the middle of so much love and resentment but had no idea how to go about it.

When we were saying our goodbyes, l was sure he had noticed my red eyes and my silence the entire tour. He looked at me and said, "My child, some wars are not yours to fight because "they aren't yours to fight." That statement made me angrier, hurt and sad because I still could not ask him any of the questions I had. Maybe if l had asked, l would have gotten satisfactory answers or perhaps not, but none of that mattered then, what was important was his efforts to spend the afternoon with me.

During my studies, l met dad again one afternoon at the library in town. He asked why l never visited him at his house, and l told him that l would never do that as long as he was staying with someone else who was not my mother. In his response, he said that as long as that was a problem l should not contact him or even think that he was my father. I took my bags and left the library. I was upset; I cried all the way home. I was so upset because for the last few months I felt like we were beginning to connect. His response wiped off all the efforts we had put into the relationship since I moved into town. It took months before we could speak to each other again.

In my final year, dad started calling and texting me. What was intriguing about these calls and texts were the messages at the end. He would say, "God bless you, my child." The first time he said it to me l was taken aback because l could not believe that my dad was giving me a blessing, something that l never thought he would ever say to me. Those short messages and calls were how we started talking to each other again though it was not very frequent and yet it became very significant to me with each call and text that came from him.

I finished school, and on my graduation day l called dad and told him to get ready for the graduation. On that day dad was looking very smart. I had never seen him wearing a suit and looking that elegant. Abruptly, he got a phone call, and when he came back to me, he told me that he could not attend the ceremony anymore. I could not even ask him why because I was overwhelmed with so much pain and all I did was accept it and walked out to the car where mum and my cousin sister were waiting. I simply got into the car and started crying uncontrollably. Mum got out of the vehicle and spoke to him, and we drove off. The whole ceremony I kept crying each time I thought about it because I thought for once in my life my dad would attend an event that had to do with me and show his support. The next day I left the city with my mum and I did not talk to him after that. My anger towards him increased, and I never called or texted as we used to when I was in college.

Two weeks before the horrific accident that claimed his life, he called me for the first time and asked me to give him $20 to assist with the hospital bills for his younger brother who was very ill at the time. I told him I did not have money and yet I did. I called my mum, angry that dad dared to call me after he had stood me up on my graduation day. Regrettably, I let my anger cloud my judgment and reason. If only I had been rational I would have given him the money and also opened a channel of communication.

On Thursday, the 21st of April 2016 when we were paying our last respects to him, I looked at his lifeless body as it laid in that coffin in a very lovely suit. My eyes were filled with tears; I was filled with all sorts of emotions of guilt, love for him and anger. I kept asking him to forgive me for having been such a terrible child. I never thought such a day would come that I had to say goodbye to him. All the anger and resentment I had towards dad was overpowered by the love I had for him at that moment.

The picture of my father lifeless, stayed with me for a long time until I consulted a counselor. The counselor made me realize what the word of God meant about honoring our parents. It was never stated when it's appropriate to honor our parents. He also made me realize that all the resentment and my actions towards him were only natural given the prevailing circumstances. The many questions I had were never answered because the best person to have solved them was long gone.

Through those counseling sessions, l realized my dad, and I loved each other. I also started realizing how my resentment and anger had also affected my character as a person. I had become a quick-tempered person and no longer trusted people easily. The way l interacted with strangers at times was very much unacceptable. It was through counseling l realized my weaknesses and started working on them.

Since then, I have managed to help some ladies going through daddy issues to cope and have encouraged others to seek counseling. Some were hesitant because in our Zimbabwean culture one does not necessarily seek professional counseling. I am happy that l managed to go for counseling. It really changed my perception and helped me heal and forgive both my dad and me.

The tour in Bulawayo with my dad, the way he dressed up for my graduation, all the phone calls/text messages and him letting me know he was my father taught me some lessons. People hurting each other and avoiding each other is and all but vanity. In Ecclesiastes 1:2, "Vanity of vanities, says the Preacher, vanity of vanities, all is vanity." Or "Everything is meaningless," says the Teacher, "utterly meaningless!" It is indeed meaningless; it is of no value so rather live every day like it was your last with that person, try harder to make peace, make an effort to focus on positive things so that tomorrow will not consume you with regret.

I was given a chance to make things right, but l did not utilize the opportunity entirely. Instead, l thought that l had the time and l was fine without him, but there is a season for everything. Ecclesiastes 3:8 talks about a time to love, and a time to hate; a time of war and a time of peace. The whole chapter shows that there is a time for everything under the sun. I failed to utilize fully my chance to reconnect with dad. I could have managed it differently by visiting him; we could have created common ground and be vulnerable to each other. But instead we both put up our walls and were defensive trying to protect ourselves and yet by so doing we only pushed each other further apart.

I managed to forgive my dad and l love him so much. It is a pity l never got the chance to tell him in person. The cherished memories l have, are those when he tried to connect with me. I have also forgiven myself for not trying hard enough to have a proper relationship with him.

I now know that I had my expectations as a child; I have come to realize that one cannot judge without all the facts. My father might have been struggling with the distance and disconnection which was there between us too. I sometimes guess all that is needed is the courage to have that difficult conversation. I want to encourage anyone who has a strained relationship with a parent or parents to consider working on rebuilding that relationship now. You are not in charge of time, and for that reason, you cannot afford to keep on fighting and causing each other unnecessary pain and grief. Instead, it is best to try to work it out. There is no gain in holding on to what the other person has done or should have done instead enjoy the moment, make peace and live a healthy life filled with love. Resentment and anger cause illnesses, something which can be avoided.

Today I am determined to do my best to make peace with everyone and to be good to them regardless of situations. I know how it feels to lose someone you love dearly and yet had succumbed to hating and resenting them for whatever reason. God loves us, He forgives us every day, and so we can all do the same for each other.

May God continue to bless my mum's soul and give her more wisdom for she played a significant role in molding our love and respect for dad. It was very easy for mum to have turned us entirely against dad by saying all the negative things about him to us. It is amazing how she does it. Up to date, she has nothing but positive things to say about dad. As a reminder of his love mum gave me his pajamas that she had kept, and she told me always to smile whenever l wore them because dad was a very cheerful, sweet and loving man when she married him. My mum's approach to life was to build, and if more people would be like her, maybe some relationships will be restored instead of being wrecked as they are today.

Chido Kusena

Chido Kusena is a production manager for Orgfert, a fertilizer manufacturing company in Harare, Zimbabwe. She has a degree in Applied Biology and Biochemistry. She is passionate about the welfare of orphans, and she often visits the orphanages whenever her schedules allow. Chido has been visiting orphanages since 2008 when she was in high school. When not glued to a screen watching a movie, she spends her time reading novels or motivational books. She also enjoys spending time with friends going on adventures. Currently, Chido is enrolled in a Senior Management Development program at the University of Zimbabwe.

To connect with Chido:

chidopkusena@yahoo.com

https://www.facebook.com/chido.kusena

The Unfurling Music Instrument Player

By Anna Nhari

It is not done until I say so!

Life's circumstances are some of the limitations that can rob a person's potential of moving forward and, improve a lifestyle and remain in a rut if it is not unraveled earlier along the journey of life. Family life situations, cultural beliefs and, society, often dictate what we can or cannot do. There is no fine line to define the limitations blame game, under the few circumstances mentioned above.

Limitations tend to prevent you from making your own decisions. Failure to make your own decisions is also attributed to culture. The words "You will bring shame to the family!", Always echo in my mind. When culture puts certain restrictions in life, one finds it difficult to fulfill certain desires and ambitions one might have from childhood. If allowed and helped along the way as they grow to develop those desires, there is a good chance that dreams are fulfilled, and one is accepted in their family, community, and culture. Most of us have specific aspirations that were abolished resulting in us being grounded. We got stuck in self-pity and could not attempt to take risks of trial and error towards an achievement because of fear that it might not be acceptable in society. Cultural norms affected so much of our choices in career paths, social preferences, marriage and a lot more if one was not influenced or supported by parents. Certain careers were frowned upon, the comments other people and parents made left you feeling discouraged. Parents needed to guide, accept, educate children to become friendly, happy and stable.

This was the story of my life, l remained in rudimentary space for years feeding on self-pity. There was no shedding off old habits of what had been cultivated in me by culture. I could not take any risks of taking on and venture into a career that was not acceptable to an African girl child while l remained within my society and the cultural system in which l grew up in. The support of family, culture, and society was too far to reach because of fear of rejection and the exaggerated gender stereotypes which were restrictive practices between men and women. The gender roles in African society are usually defined and based on historical roles and backgrounds set for men and women in a cultural setting. Up to this day, gender roles are so important in my culture; this made it difficult for me because l had to wait long enough for my adult transformation to take place in my area of interest. I liked playing an instrument, yet I stayed stuck in despair always contemplating and feeding on the same unproductive patterns yet going nowhere. Is it true that our past informs our future? Yes. That is the journey l embarked on - carrying excess baggage of wishful thinking *(dai ndine mapapiro – if I had wings, I'd fly)* into my future then.

As an African girl child in the 1960s, culture also played a significant role in which l had to believe, live and remain in its boundaries. It was so important for my family and society.

It was unheard of that a girl child would play a musical instrument. If that were to happen there would be an uproar in the family and community. It was taboo. Traditionally, only men played musical instruments such as drums, *mbira* (thumb piano) and bhosvo (Trumpet) while women danced. Besides, our parents never listened to nor identified our needs, which resulted in my further frustration and stagnation. It was the belief and still is believed by our indigenous African elders not to encourage a girl to play musical instruments. They associated this with consequent bad behavior, promiscuity which could compromise her future.

I really loved music and more so playing an instrument. I yearned for it more and more especially when l moved to the United Kingdom. The visibility of women in the music industry helped me take on my transformation slowly but surely. I needed to make choices in planning for the future. I was getting advanced in age, and my children had left the nest. I needed to make choices that would not only be a dream but would also help weave my future into reality. It meant a willingness to change some gender roles and programming influenced by society. It involved breaking certain limitations, beliefs about the cultural boundaries, dealing with long-grown shame, derisive comments from colleagues and my community. I had to think of challenges ahead as l could not read or write music notes. I needed to find someone to help and advise me on what to do.

On the other hand, l still had the cultural gender norms inkling at the back of my mind, the African cultural norms that had shaped me for years. Let me point out, the issue of gender roles is not only in African society. According to an article by Pennsylvania State University, "Many gender roles around the world were dictated by the environment and needs of society."

After looking at all these cultural aspects, l decided to embark on a journey to do my own research in what choice of musical instrument to play. I experienced a major chrysalis moment of my life, which needed me to be quiet and still and know that there was God, my creator who allows choices. It strengthened me although I did not know how long it was going to take, or which direction to follow, let alone the outcome.

I started talking to those who play musical instruments, seeking advice on how to go about selecting a musical instrument to play. As I listened to their responses, it sounded complicated and quite involved. I had given up on my dream of ever playing an instrument...It was like a joke listening to the seasoned players as they demonstrated playing, the instruments. My age provoked mixed feelings, which weighed down on my confidence. However, at that stage I felt like l was in transition. It was time for me to reflect, observe and then implement a plan although l feared the stigma attached to playing an instrument at old age. However, the power to change and fulfill my dream dominated.

I felt challenged by South African born musicians like Miriam Makeba, Hugh Masekela, and Zimbabwean born Stella Chiweshe, who made it through hard times, in exile. I neither knew how long it took to learn how to play an instrument nor the outcome. I took a stride at a time unhurriedly and reminded myself that my brain was still good enough to learn new things. I needed to be calm in order to make a sensible decision in choosing the right instrument to play. I did not know the costs involved in acquiring the instrument as well as how many lessons I would need. Finally, I had made up my mind regarding instrument of choice, but my dilemma was to choose between a guitar and a ukulele, a small four-stringed guitar of Hawaiian origin.

Having given it much research and thought, I chose the ukulele. I knew little about it. I found it fascinating especially when the sales representative demonstrated how to play the instrument. There were so many positive comments about the ukulele. Most of there were on YouTube channels. The good reviews gave me more confidence although at the back of my mind I was going through feelings of self-doubt and debating on whether it was worth the time and money investing in that little instrument. It is also a careless belief when people say if you never learned to play an instrument at a young age you may not make it later in life. Let alone imagining walking into a music shop and buying one. See! The patterns of limitation crept up again inviting setbacks. I had to fight it. I reminded myself that when I went to school music was not offered in our curriculum. Once again, that was just finding justification to abandon my project. I recalled what Dr. Roy Ernest, founder of New Horizon said, "People of any age can learn to play and gain a level of satisfaction." I went ahead with my choice and bought the ukulele. I did not have the foggiest idea of how to begin to play it. It was the most humbling thing l had ever done in my life at that adult age.

The acquisition of the ukulele instrument was extremely exciting even before l got to play it. It was a significant step forward. I had overcome one of the most harmful huddles that prevent most people from reaching their highest potential.

Now that l had the instrument l felt like l had added a new creation to my time on earth. I could not wait to get home and work on practicing my instrument. I realized that l did not know how to tweak or play chords. I had imagined it to be as easy as buying it, yet there was so much to learn, this included, how to handle the instrument, tune it and learn the chords to practice them.

It felt like l was putting little effort on how to play the instrument at first. I quickly got very frustrated as l discovered learning to play the ukulele difficult, and technically challenging without any immediate reward. I had to learn to have resilience, patience, and endurance and to work harder while encouraging myself not to quit. The problem was that l wanted instant results. There are no shortcuts in learning to play an instrument, such as the Ukulele. I reminded myself that nothing good came easy. I needed to dedicate more time to practice all the nitty-gritty that came along with playing an instrument. It meant more practice, concentration, and dedication. Since l had no teacher or a known group of ukulele players l could join, l learned to fingerpick and strumming patterns from the user-friendly YouTube lessons.

I do not have a good voice yet playing goes well with singing to the instruments. I had to learn the hard way. My progress was slow, but l learned to sing while jamming along as well. I could not see the little progress l was making because l chose to remain stuck in a rut of self-criticism. I often felt terrible and afraid of failure which reminded me of my childhood. There was no room for failure.

With time l learned that practice and discipline were recipes for producing good music and a good instrument player. I decided to have a few lessons from a music school just to learn the basics. Each time l came out of practice l felt good and wanted to do more. I squeezed out every extra penny I had to keep up with the lessons and not miss out. It was expensive l must say, but I needed to make a sacrifice for my dream to come true. After a few lessons, I was on my own. When l told my friends that l was learning to play an instrument, they would often respond with, "You are now mad to do so at your age. What has gone wrong with you?" but I had already discovered that it is not too late to start for those who yearn to learn to play an instrument.

With time, the drive to play a piece of music got me out to meet other people who kept me going. I started going out where musicians performed just to listen and get the feel of seeing others on stage. I was encouraged and motivated by what l saw and felt l would one day be on that stage. That meant l did not want my transformation to dry up by being exposed to elements of failure. Instead, l watered it with music and practice to help it develop and fly. I often referred my journey to Life Chrysalis because it truly went through the stages a beautiful butterfly goes through. As I kept that in mind, it encouraged me to continue working hard and maintain my commitment. It was painful at first strumming the strings. I developed calloused fingers, but the pain was only temporary.

Slowly and confidently I was playing more using chords to the extent of writing chords for certain pieces of music in my language of Ndebele and Shona. I got more incentives from listening and playing along ukulele songs. I also experimented with some of the songs in my dialect as l went along. Today l am now being invited to churches to play with seasoned players, at women conferences and other functions. I play in a few care homes although I find it a bit challenging because I need to learn to sing songs relevant to their generation.

My research and experience have taught me many social and health benefits of learning to play an instrument at an adult age. As the old saying goes, "The distance between dreaming and reality is called taking action." That is what l did. I took action, and the decisions and challenges of undertaking this particular move made me stronger. The brain was awakened to new challenges. It gave me the potential to meet other people, who have become social connections from different walks of life.

As I concentrate and focus on playing and singing, it has assisted me in applying the same skills in other areas of my life. I am overjoyed and filled with love and peace. I feel the whole process helped me remove all the silk and frass surrounding my life transformation into becoming a beautiful butterfly.

Playing an instrument gives me purpose and meaning of living my life in a magical moment. It has enhanced my skill in writing and performance. There are benefits that l never recognized before today. My life has been enriched so much, in fact to the extent of boosting my confidence and self-esteem.

I have so far met a few musicians who help me so much with creativity that l am no longer solitary and confined to my home since my children left home. That move has resulted in meeting great friends and has helped me open up and be authentic as l engage in discussions. I am now able to express myself through playing an instrument and singing. My social skills have also improved, and l can engage in conversations easily.

As we all know, music embraces and brings together cultures from known and unknown different parts of the world. I have also realized that musical instruments and music have become a large-scale universal language, which individuals use to communicate. It enhances and stimulates one's mental and physical memory and experience. Like I mentioned before, there is great pleasure in playing an instrument to both the musician and the listeners.

There is a lot that goes on around musical instrument players and their instruments like guitar, drums, ukuleles, recorders, pianos, wind instruments, violin, and percussions to name a few. Playing instruments is quite rewarding and naturally brings in some relaxing moments

Picking up and playing an instrument helps reduce stress, increases productivity and develops creativity. You live a healthy and happier life. It also gives a sense of accomplishment and a high pleasure in just sitting there holding your instrument and producing a sound that is good or composing a piece worth listening. Playing an instrument has a powerful pull on our emotions. I often sense it. It has undoubtedly helped me boost my mood, my self-esteem, and well-being whether I am playing my instrument or playing someone else's piece. It is believed that it makes one become stable and exercise more empathy about others. It increases your listening skills, making you a better listener in tuning, in expressions as well as in conversing with others in general. I have been inspired to create or practice more pieces of music. You also find that a particular piece can make you happy and relax, sad or cry

While learning to read and write musical chords, organizational skills, time management for practice, record keeping of notes, patience and mastering what you have learned is of the essence. An instrument helps you unwind after a hard day's work. I am on a journey of having my music recorded.

This process has been a rewarding journey and experience. I have bypassed the cultural boundaries which limited me from my dream. I surely encourage adults out there to take on an instrument. A ukulele is fun and melodious instrument. Its small size is inviting and not so intimidating when compared to a guitar. Those who used to laugh at me are now my audience and admirers. It is never too late. What started as a dead road has become the beginning of a clear, safe path to drive my life on. The ukulele has inspired me and changed my life.

I look forward to massive changes ahead of me.

Anna Nhari

Anna Nhari was born and grew up in Africa where cultural vices during her generation, limited women from learning to play musical instruments. It was after when she migrated to the United Kingdom that she managed to pursue her dream, which landed her into composing music and playing the ukulele at church and public settings. Occasionally, she plays in collaboration with other musicians.

Anna is an integrative counselor who has been trained to use different approaches to counseling. These approaches help people to unravel and find a healthy perception about themselves, to bring a healing process in their experience of traumatic and stressful situations. Anna co-authored a book on resilience which has been well received by the general public.

Outside of professional interests, she enjoys computing and designs indoor gardens for whoever needs that service and even for the benefit of supporting general health and mental well-being.

To contact Anna:

nhariana@yahoo.com

https://www.facebook.com/anna.nhari

How I Survived Abuse And Thrived

By Kamla Dasrath

I thought my life was complete; I had met my prince charming. He was loving, caring and he paid what I thought was a lot of attention. I attributed a lot of what was happening as part of the honeymoon period. However, all that would soon change, but in sharing my story, I would like my readers to know that this is not about blaming anyone but about a woman's journey who has achieved a lot through self-discovery. I was by no means a perfect wife; I had my issues with childhood abuse which he held against me. I learned so much about relationship struggles that women face. My experience gave me a serious look at the challenges men face because of societal expectations. Society expects men to be in control, manage their work, household and provide for their family. There is also the part where I acknowledge the role of women in encouraging some of that behavior. There is quite a lot to consider when looking at anyone's character, and there is that part where who we are is influenced by childhood experiences, trauma in one form or another. The trouble is when we grow older, we expect every adult to be whole. I am hoping that by sharing my journey, I will be able to help someone avoid the pitfalls which I experienced.

My work environment was male-dominated, and every day he asked me which one of my colleagues I had slept with. I thought he was jealous because he loved me so much. I can't believe I bought all that nonsense. I guess deep down I knew that something was fundamentally wrong with my relationship, but for whatever reason, I was determined to make my marriage work. I did not want to fail or to be alone. I made excuses to myself for his behavior. I just brushed off all those comments as insecurity. I thought if I tried harder to show him that I was honest, sincere, and loved him with all my heart, I would gain his trust and he would be nice to me.

Before moving to Florida, I quit my well-paying Wall Street job and high-stress lifestyle. My husband also quit his six-figure high-stress job in New York. I came from the corporate world, Citibank and Wall Street and I left that to get married. I wanted six kids, the white picket fence, and it all seemed just perfect. I studied Chinese medicine, Astrology and Energy Healing. I started a Gift Basket business, and I volunteered with support groups, He even encouraged me to invest in the stock market to keep busy.

My marriage started as a dream; I could not believe I had been so lucky to meet such an amazing man. I was swept off my feet instantly, but this did not last. The trouble was, I did not think there was a problem.

After I quit my job and moved to Florida, he would call me at home several times a day. I saw that as love and caring.

I thought it was him missing me, until I realized he was checking up on me.

I guess I had not realized that over time I had been isolated from my family, friends, and anyone who cared about me. Moving away from New York seemed like a good idea at the time. I was happy to be a stay at home wife. The best thing was getting away from the stress. Starting a family, we tried to get pregnant, for a few years but it wasn't working. All the doctor visits created their own set of problems and tensions. We finally decided to go for an In vitro Fertilization procedure (IVF), a medical procedure whereby an egg is fertilized by sperm in a test tube or elsewhere outside the body. Both of us had to go through several tests, with all the very costly procedures. The whole process was very stressful.

Even though my husband made me feel like he was doing me a favor, I was very grateful. He hated the whole process, but the need to become a mother blinded me with all the hormone shots, I didn't realize he didn't want to have a baby. The experience my body went through was unimaginable, not to mention the emotional torture but I was determined to keep trying, and…that was my life for nine years.

I remember when I worked at Wall Street, I usually took the ferry to and from work on the East River, I can't tell you how many times I wanted to jump overboard and end it all. Those thoughts should have sounded the alarm bells. I kept thinking that I was married, and had everything I wanted, then why did I feel confused and out of my mind. I could not live that lie; but I could not tell anyone what was truly going on. I did not think there was a name to the type of abuse, constant criticism, cynicism, and the disrespect I was getting from my husband. I strongly believed that it was all my fault…if only I could be a better wife.

After failing to conceive, I decided to be open to other options, and adoption was one of them. A friend talked to me about adopting in India, and I traveled there to look into the process.

When 9/11(September 11th Twin Tower bombing) happened, I was in the middle of IVF. At that time, my husband's seven-year-old cousin lost her grandmother who was looking after her. She ended up in an orphanage. We canceled the IVF procedures and focused on adopting his cousin. Adopting a 7-year-old was a big challenge mainly because the agency instructed us not to get too close or create a bond with her in case the adoption didn't go through. I studied everything I could find about being a new parent, taking adoption courses but my husband was not interested; and he did not want to attend the classes.

Soon after the adoption, the stock market crashed. My husband's job relocated several hours away and he could not find work. We had a mortgage, bills and a loan to pay back for the adoption. Now we also had an additional member to our family. We then decided to start our construction business. I was thrown into unfamiliar territory. With the stress which I already had, then running a company where I had no prior experience of running a business before was a struggle. I had to learn everything. Throughout the adoption process, the stress at home had escalated. When our daughter came home, he was not around for her; he spent more time at work. I had to accept that I was living as a single mom.

So how did my life end up like that?! How did I end up at 49, financially dependent and in a destructive relationship? The stressful life caused several health crises. I decided to focus on my needs, my health, and my daughter. The business was ours, not mine; I felt trapped. After watching my relationship and my health deteriorate, I decided right there and then, to immerse myself in absolutely everything that had to do with changing my health and lifestyle. It was the right time to take control of my life!

After I began to take care of my health, I gained confidence and a sense of purpose; my foggy mind started to get clearer. I started reading self-help books. I read books about problem marriages and how to avoid divorce. I went on YouTube, Google any website I could find. I needed answers because I had been living in my head for too long. While I was in the nutrition course, one of the ladies mentioned the word "gaslighting," and it stuck in my head. After class and in between work I spent many hours researching about mental health and abuse which opened a whole new world of Narcissists and Psychopaths.

I could not believe the traits they were describing; I was struck by Sam Vaknin a professor of psychology who shares from a narcissist's point of view. Everything became more evident, "he is like Jackal and Hyde," that was my first thought. This was my experience earlier in the marriage. Living with a person who has narcissistic behavior is like being in a fog, and that explained why I struggled to find value in what I was doing. I was made to feel like I was always at fault. There were no flashing red lights; people with such traits are very smart with their actions. From one minute to the next, they make you feel so happy go lucky in love (making future-plans) the next you want to jump off the nearest bridge.

I didn't know if I was losing my mind and seeing things. I kept asking myself, "what is wrong with me?" Labeling is not my style, but how could I be so blind? I learned that…It was a game to them; you are not a real person but just a thing they believe they own. What would a normal person do, when someone they love, says to them, "When I am done with you, no one will want you!" At the time I did not understand what he meant. I was busy trying to be a better wife doing everything to please him, but his statement also brought a cold chill down my spine. His whole demeanor changed when he reached that point. He looked at me with pure hatred. I felt horrible.

Looking back, I'm very grateful that I did not get pregnant by him doing the IVF. I learned that the stress from the relationship affected the child in the womb, I discovered that the pressure I was going through, would have definitely affected the development of the baby, most of the time I was a nervous wreck. I did not want to bring a child into this world that way, so through the whole process, that was a concern at the back of my mind. The environment was too toxic.

I realized that all the red flags were right there from the time we started dating, the lies, the manipulation and lack of empathy. What a difference it would have made, if I had come across a book or information that brought awareness. This is something that is found across cultures, and both men and women can have narcissistic tendencies. I say this though, I am not giving a diagnosis, but I know what I went through for 30 years of marriage. I am sharing my own experiences and only recently understood what was happening after many years of enduring the abuse.

I am determined to help other women walk into relationships well informed. I will have achieved my life purpose if my story helps just one woman to avoid wasting their life with a partner whose mental disposition causes so much pain to others. If they decide to stay, they will know how to protect their emotions and health.

According to experts, there are warning signs which you should pay attention to. The list is much longer than this. I have listed only 12. Please pay attention, as this might save your life and your sanity. When you get to know and understand who you are dealing with, you must be careful; seek help if necessary. The main thing to remember is that, there is nothing WRONG WITH YOU!

<u>Here are 12 red flags to look for:</u>

1. You feel on-edge and unsettled around this person, but you still want to be with them.

You ignore some of the behaviors which makes you uncomfortable and are in constant competition for their attention.

2. They withhold affection and undermine your self-esteem.

Praise and flatter you and quickly seem uninterested.

3. Love bombing, over texting and calling, giving you compliments on social media - making you feel you are on cloud nine within a short space

of time in the relationship. You start to rely on them for the source of confidence.

4. He compares you to everyone else in their life.

-Ex-lovers, friends, family members elevating you then eventually your replacement, then later devalue you with hurtful comparisons.

5. Lies and excuses, they have reasons for everything, even things that do not require explanations. They will always blame others; they rationalize their behavior rather than improving it.

6. Insult you with a condescending, joking sort of attitude.

Teasing becomes the primary mode and way of communication in your relationship. They subtly belittle your intelligence and achievements. If you point this out, they will call you hypersensitive and crazy.

7. Surround themselves with former lovers and potential mates.

Brags that their exes find them irresistible and still want to sleep with him/her but assures you that there is nothing for you to worry about. They want to feel like they are in demand and this will make you jealous.

8. Accuses you of emotions that they are intentionally provoking, just to upset you. They will blatantly flirt with their ex in your face, or on social media for the world to see if you complain they will call you needy.

9. You will find yourself explaining the basic elements of human respect to a full-grown man/woman.

Reasonable people understand the fundamental concepts of honesty and kindness.

10. The Ultimate hypocrite.

They have incredibly high expectations of fidelity, respect, and adoration. After the idealization phase, they will give none of this back to you, they will cheat, lie, insult and degrade, but you are expected to remain respectful.

11. Gaslighting.

Blatantly denies their own manipulative behavior and ignores evidence when confronted with it. They will become outraged if you attempt to disprove their delusions with facts.

12. Your feelings.

After a run-in with a psychopath, you will feel insane, exhausted, drained, shocked, suicidal, and empty. You will tear apart your entire life, spending money, ending friendships, and searching for some sort of reason behind it all.

There are more than 30 traits, in 30 years of marriage I was probably at the receiving end of most them.

The best decision ever!

While looking into colleges and career choices for my daughter, I discovered the Institute for Integrative Nutrition (IIN). Attending the world's largest nutrition school allowed me to balance my job of running a full-time heavy equipment construction business with online study at IIN and choosing to make my health a priority.

Looking back, I can see how my experiences have not only taught me great lessons but brought me full circle. Now that I am in my fifties, I know that living a healthy lifestyle, and caring for our mind, body, and soul is the most important thing we can do for ourselves and our loved ones.

Significant changes like gardening, growing organic, non-GMO fruits and vegetables and shopping at the local farmers' markets, mean so much. You definitely need to "be the change you want to see."

From studying astrology, natural medicine, and proper nutrition, to learning more about Feng Shui, religion and spirituality, I understand that life is not "one size fits all." We must choose our own path and respect each other's choices.

This is what I now do… I am helping other women to rebuild their lives by taking control and make healthy choices, to enjoy better health, relationships and live an incredible, exceptional life.

You can start over at any age; just know that your life does not have to end.

Now I help other women to:

-Develop compassion

-Create healthy boundaries

-Find their happiness

-Connect with their intuition

-End drama cycles and harmful patterns

-Honor their truth

-Develop deep, meaningful relationships.

-Rewrite their story

-Feel empowered and excited about the future

-Raise self-esteem and self-confidence

-Gain a healthy lifestyle

-Feel complete without needing external validation.

My life struggles sent me on a mission, and I ended up finding my purpose. Even though at the time it seemed as if my life had ended, I was pushed to take a hard look at myself and asked myself the question, "Why was I here?" I went on a quest to find out. I am glad that I am here now, where I am at peace with my life and experiences and everyone who has been part of it to this point. We have gotten past the anger and can work together constructively; we enjoy our separate lives, and also respect the fact that we are different.

I got my life back when I actively looked for answers and intentionally looked for solutions, healing, and personal growth. It takes time to build your strength. Seek your purposes, volunteer your time to help those less privileged; it puts things into perspective. Find a support group, read, give your mind something to be excited about. Map out how you want to move forward. At least if you decide to stay, you will be able to protect your emotions, create healthy boundaries, and your life will not be spiraling down in a free fall. You will have control of your life.

We aspire together; we achieve together for the betterment of ourselves, our planet and the universe. What makes life so rich are the different situations we experience. Some of them are amazing blessings and others just happen to be lessons.

I know that by adopting a healthier lifestyle and sharing my knowledge with others is a win-win choice. Life should not be about separation or divide and conquer; it's about togetherness.

By taking control of your life, and making healthy choices, we can enjoy better health and live an incredible, fulfilling, exceptional life.

Kamla Dasrath

Kamla Dasrath was born in the Caribbean Island of Trinidad & Tobago; she moved to the United States from Canada in 1970. She grew up and worked in New York City, her last job in New York was with City Bank on Wall Street. When Kamla got married and moved to Florida, she started a construction company with her husband and still manages it today.

As a teenager, Kamla studied Feng Shui and Astrology, and as an adult, she trained in Holistic nutrition, Energy healing, Reiki and EFT Emotional freedom technique an alternative treatment for physical pain and emotional distress.

It's also referred to as tapping or psychological acupressure. She uses all the knowledge and skills she acquired in her current business, as a health and relationship mentor.

During her spare time Kamla enjoys comedy and making everyone relax with humor, she loves gardening

cooking and researching, Religions and Natural healing from all over the world.

Connect with Kamla:

http://holisticintuitivenutrition.com/

https://www.facebook.com/groups/HealthyRelationshipWithKamla/

Know Your Worth

By Monica Kunzekweguta

I have been accused of many things in my adult life, including being a no-nonsense, confident, independent woman. I remember my elderly great aunt looking at me smiling, and saying, "umm you fancy yourself too much that's why you are still single at the age of 30." I guess she was on the same page as those people who know me, my friends and family, who said, "your standards are too high that's why you won't find a man." After hearing it so many times, I finally conceded, lowered my standards thinking maybe, just maybe I was the problem. I started a relationship with Tom; we met at a friend's birthday party. He was handsome, charming and intelligent. That was the worst mistake that I ever made. It didn't take long before I realized I had landed myself in hot soup.

We started dating. I experienced what is called love-bombing, with him showering me with so much love within a short space of time. I was in cloud 99. I got hooked, and when I was comfortable in the relationship and had started trusting him, that's when he began revealing his true colors, which as you might have guessed had a nasty element to them. What I saw and experienced made me realized that to some extent my life had been so protected that I was out of touch with real life issues or challenges that other women deal with every day in their relationships. I had talked to my friend Vikki; we grew up together in Manicaland, a province in Zimbabwe. I would tell her about the cheating, the emotional and verbal abuse I was being subjected to. In my entire life, I had never come across a man who sulked, folded his arms like a toddler, threw a tantrum, and not talk to me for days, only to then break the silence when it suited him. He used a lot of threatening language. Unfortunately for him, I did not take kindly to threats, and I did not want to live my life in uncertainty.

Despite some of these challenges, I stayed in the relationship hoping things would change until one day I was about to use his mobile phone when a message came through WhatsApp (Mobile App used for sending text/voice messages). I was horrified to see a half-naked photo of a nurse; I believe it was a nurse because of the uniform. I was disgusted. I immediately deleted the message and used the phone to make the call. I did not make a fuss about the photo because at that point I had seen enough and had decided to end the relationship with him. Being with someone like that was not going to be my portion in life. I guess the lady wherever she was, was waiting for some response from Tom. Unfortunately, she never got any response because he never saw the nasties, I made sure of that. It didn't take much for her to figure out that I was responsible. She didn't know what I had done with the photo and threatened to sue me if the picture ended up on a public platform. However, that was not my character. Unlike her, I had the dignity to maintain. Her, like most people who act before they think, they forget that once they press the send button, they are no longer in control of what happens to their photos or the message they shared.

I told my friend Vikki that I was going to end the relationship. I was not prepared to waste my life working on building my confidence and self-esteem which was continually being chipped away by a man like Tom.

"I have better and greater things to work on," I told her. Vikki had on numerous occasions shared the challenges and abuse she was facing in her marriage. I could not believe that all the 20 years of her marriage had been such a struggle. I found it depressing that she expected her marriage to improve only by prayer and fasting.

My question is, and has always been, why should it be so hard to be with someone? There has been a lot of cases of violence and spousal murders reported in recent years, and I struggle to get my head around it all. As for me, I will never try to fit in again, and I sure will never lower my standards to accommodate anyone. If the shoe size is wrong, it only means one thing, the shoe is not supposed to be mine period, and I won't force my foot into it!

"But Mona, how do you do it? I want to know how you do it?" Vikki had asked me, and there was an emphatic tone to her question. I knew what she was talking about. I got a sense that she had spent some time processing it.

"Do what?" I asked to make sure we were on the same page. "How do you manage to leave an abusive relationship and switch off as if nothing happened? Most of us struggle. We hang in there and do what we know best, pray, meditate, and hope, expecting the man to change."

At the time I did not know if that was a compliment or not because single women are not celebrated that much in our culture, especially at my age when they do not have children. It seems to magnify their failures. After listening to her for a few minutes, I realized that she was curious and sincere. Vikki wanted to know for sure. I had done a bit retrospect of my own a while back and had asked myself why I generally do not put up with uncomfortable situation especially where men are concerned.

I remember Tom asking me with an expression of disgust on his face after

I pointed out that I didn't tolerate the lies and cheating at any level.

"So where do you think you will find a man who will not cheat on you? I don't know what your problem is because I have never hit you!"

"Everyone is different," I told him. "I do not have the extra energy to teach an adult life's fundamental concepts of honesty, kindness, respect, and fidelity. Respect is something taught to us as kids so that when we become adults, we know how to treat others."

When he was in one of his rude and irritable moods, I would say to him; "The all that's attractive about you goes out the window. Whenever a handsome or a beautiful person shows their ugliness through their words and actions, it erases all their positive attributes such as their handsomefullness and beautifulness. Unfortunately, once these positive attributes have been deleted, they rarely get restored, not to their original state anyway."

So, for me that was what killed it, the apologies after each episode failed to wash off the tainted picture which I now carried.

In my relationship with Tom, I lived in fear of what would happen if he hit me. So far, he had been verbally and emotionally abusive. The chances were, I would have retaliated and ended up in trouble with the law. Sometimes, I felt that the verbal abuse was an attempt to push me to the edge. I kept taking it in and taking it in and had bottled up too much. I could feel it. However, my message to him was clear, if you keep chipping away at something, eventually it would break. It took Tom under 18 months to do enough damage; I was done!

"Well, this is what you get when you try to please people and lower your standards!" I thought.

I can safely say I have been both protected and defended by men from the moment I arrived on this earth. The first being my father. I think when he and my Mum divorced, he made it his mission to protect me and made me his priority. I also believe that if he knew the conditions and the regulations of the church he later joined, he might not have joined it. To this day, the church believes the girl child is only meant for marriage, be a wife and have babies. It's a community which seems to have everything designed to give men the best of what life has to offer. Those who are born and raised in that church know nothing else otherwise. So, I guess my view will sound absurd to them. The girl child seems to long for nothing but being married into polygamy. Even if it means going head first into untold poverty. It's a case of Hakuna Matata (no worries) even when surrounded by hunger, high child and mother mortality, violence by women against other women, it is survival of the fittest. It is the sort of stuff that is not talked about as communities and authorities choose to turn a blind eye.

That's where I have always had a different perspective on my younger sisters. When I was born, my parents were not in the church; I only joined when I was about 7 years old. My father had been molding me from birth. I would hear his voice from when I was still in my mother's tummy. After their divorce, my father continued to be the strong voice that gave me reassurance, guidance, and direction. All that was instilled in me could not be undone, because it was sealed in my being and through my cells. During those formidable early years, it had been drilled into me that I was loved, valued, important, and I had rights. My father always created time for me and that made me feel special.

I was three years old when I went to live with my uncle and aunt in Mufakose, one of the oldest townships in Harare. My father had decided it was proper for me to live in a family setting where there were both a mother and a father figure. At the time he was living Bulawayo, the second largest city in Zimbabwe. As a single parent, I believe he was facing some challenges with childcare since he lived very far away from other family members.

I loved living with my aunt, uncle and cousins, but I missed my father.

One Saturday morning I was informed that baba(father) was coming to visit with a special visitor. I was excited because I was going to see him. I missed him. I had not seen him in a few weeks. My father often made the trip to Harare most Fridays, to come and see me. So, my cousins and I were told to have an early shower so that we looked presentable when they showed up. We usually had our bathe around 5 pm, just in time for getting indoors at sunset. We played outside all day, only coming indoors to eat or for a drink. But on this day, we had cleaned up by midday.

My father and his visitor, a beautiful lady dressed in a blue and white two-piece suit with matching shoes arrived around 12:30 pm. After lunch, all the kids went outside to play, as usual and I was the only one called back into the lounge to join my father and that lady. She looked a bit shy. I sat next to my father, and he started talking by reminding the woman about the conversation they had had earlier on. He looked at her and said, "do you recall the conversation we had about my daughter. Like I said earlier, she comes first, everything else is secondary including my marriage to you if it happens. I wanted you to meet her first." The lady looked at me smiled and nodded her head in acknowledgment. He continued, "take some time to think about it because I am a father first. Any decision I make right or wrong will affect my child; I have to be right this time. I have been divorced once, and you see how it affects her. I can't do this to her again, that's why I want you to know how much this young girl means to me".

He then turned to me and said, "Mona, this lady is Karen, you can call her auntie; she might come and become part of our family if she decides to marry me." My face lit up because I thought with a woman in the house, I will go and live with my father. I was happy with my uncle and auntie, but I missed my father. When the introductions were done, I went outside to play, and I was praying that she said yes. All I wanted was someone to call mum, and to have a normal family.

The conditions my father laid out to Karen might seem minor, but to me, it instilled one more message, I was a priority, and a serious decision could not be made without enough consideration of how it would affect me. I think this is where some parents fall short. A child has only his or her parents; and he or she should be a priority because they need to be fed, educated, clothed, protected and taught some life skills. I had all of that. After eight months, I was told that my father was getting married, I figured auntie Karen had said yes. After they settled, I went to live with them; I was now eight years old. I was excited, but that excitement would soon disappear.

I was happy to have a mother and a father again, but my happiness was short lived. A lot happened when my father was at work. One day by chance, it came to his attention that things were a bit tough for his little girl. We had a Civic Day at school and all the kids went to school dressed in their best clothes. Just before we left, my father noticed that I was wearing this flimsy wrinkled, pale pink cotton dress which Karen got a neighbor to make for me. She chose that dress for me to wear.

He said, "Mona go and get dressed we are going to be late."

I said, "I am already dressed."

I was standing by the door carrying my little bookcase. He wanted to know what had happened to the decent clothes he bought me a few weeks back. Although I knew I could not answer because I was terrified. He looked at Karen, but she ignored him.

My father went to my room to look for a cute dress, but there weren't any clothes in my wardrobe except for the flimsy stuff, the clothes I used at home. He looked everywhere until he went into their bedroom, searching in their closet. He still could not find them.

He came out and said, "Monica, where are all your clothes I bought?" Noticing that I was too terrified to speak, standing and fixed in one position, he went back and turned their bedroom upside down. Karen chose to ignore my father and instead started shouting at him saying that it was not his responsibility as a man to choose clothes for a girl-child to wear. My father did not respond; he kept looking until he found my clothes tucked away in an old cardboard box which was kept on top of their wardrobe where I could not reach. He took out my favorite brown and white dress which was still brand new. Although I took that dress, and wore it per his instruction, I knew I was going to pay one way or the other because it was not him I spent my days with. It was none other than Karen.

My father looked at Karen and calmly repeated his words from the introduction day, "Remember, I told you that you can not be with me if you cannot accept my child! I am all she has got."

He began to shake his head…nikisi-nikisi hazvishandiba izvi!" (no-no this doesn't work!). He continued, "When I come back from work, I want to find you gone!" He extended his hand and said, "huya mwana wangu, hande." (come on my child, let's go).

I reached for his hand, and we went to the car. I sat in the front seat, but in my heart I was praying that she gets to leave. When Karen realized the seriousness of her action, she came out running after the car as we drove off. I could see her in the review mirror. My father stopped the car and when she approached his window, she started to ask for forgiveness.

"Ndapota-pota murume wangu handichazviiti futi" (I am so sorry my husband, I will never do, it again) Karen pleaded. My father did not say much. He just insisted that he wanted her gone by the time he got back from work and that she could take anything she wanted from the house. He didn't care, he wanted her gone.

We drove from Seke to Chikwanha where our family owned a grocery store. There was a lot of traffic that day, so it took us about 40 minutes, to get Chihwanha from our house, a journey which normally took half the time. All father kept saying was, "no, no this doesn't work" and checking if I was alright, I was not brave enough to say what I was going through. I was too terrified. He was protecting me from abuse; his words were not empty words. Deep down, I was happy. I thought with Karen gone, my troubles had come to an end. Unfortunately, when we came back home that evening, Karen had called her mum to help her to intervene for her with the promise that she will change the way she treated me, she stayed.

From then on, the treatment I got improved a little bit. There were some changes but still with hidden cruelty. The treatment changed from being starved to force-feeding. As a child I used to struggle to eat, I believe most kids do. Karen would intentionally give me adult food portions and stand there beside me until I finished eating. I would eat until I was about to throw up. She didn't care but insisted that I finish my portion.

Karen was always on standby to slapping me with the back of her hand if I made any mistake, and I made a lot of those because I was nervous all the time. One day she slapped me, and I had a nose bleed. As I was going to go to the bathroom to wash the blood off, she yanked me back and said, "Where do you think you are going? Here use these newspapers to clean yourself up." I started to cry. "Don't even dare cry," she said raising her hand to give me another back of the hand slap. "I am not your mother!" she reminded me as if I didn't know.

She would openly shower me with a lot of praises in front of my father. I knew that if I had opened my mouth to say anything I would come across as an ungrateful spoiled brat. Parents should never underestimate how much their children can understand and articulate stuff. Karen has probably forgotten about her behavior, or the trauma it might have caused, but I haven't. The good part is that I have not forgotten how special my father made me feel, and it is from his love and protection, that I know that I am not supposed to be abused by anyone.

As a firstborn and first grandchild, I was loved. However, it also came with challenges and responsibilities. From as young as six all the grandchildren were encouraged to respect me. I used to find it strange that another child would address me with such respect, but I got used to it. I was also reminded that I should always be a role model for my young brothers and sisters. I took my responsibilities seriously. We did not witness any violence in the family or saw our parents arguing. I grew up to know that it should not happen. As a child, the only beating I got was at school, and at home only by Karen. My father never knew about the beatings. My father, uncles, aunties or grandmothers never laid a hand on me. So, the question I ask a man who threatens to hit me is…

"What have you contributed to my well-being so far, that gives you the right to hit me or tear me apart?"

Besides, I feel I would have let my young brothers and sisters down. What would I tell them if I intentionally stay in an abusive relationship, how would I guide them and encourage them to keep safe?

The other person who taught me that, a loving relationship was not achieved through manipulation, and guilt-tripping was my first love. We respected each other and wanted the best for each other. He respected my choices, and I also respected him. He was kind, gentle, generous and protective. We often got in trouble for doing the right thing. He would come to our house to ask for permission to take me out, despite all our efforts to do everything by the book we got punished for it, but that is a story to tell for another day. After experiencing the quality of friendship, I had with him; I could not see myself in a relationship where there was no respect for one another. I knew I could not be someone else's doormat.

Unfortunately, my first love had to go abroad to further his studies, other forces came into play, and the relationship ended. From that relationship, I learned that it was possible to be with someone who compliments you and make life beautiful and worthwhile. I am grateful I had the opportunity to have such an experience. I know when I am not treated right. Other people go through life without ever meeting that person who ticks all the right boxes.

Yes, I seem to be praising men only, but in my experience, men have played a pivotal role in shaping who I am today. My uncle Walter (May his soul rest in peace) used to take my sister, Judith and I, to his workplace. At the time, my sister was in grade 9, and I was in grade 10, in preparation take my final exams. Uncle Walter was the Production Manager for Caridon, the largest sandpaper producing company in Africa at the time. On arrival at his workplace, he would give us some dust coats and assign us some homework. He would pop in to check how we were doing; have tea breaks and lunch with us. This was frowned upon by most men in that organization as it was a male-dominated industry. Witnessing Uncle Walter paying so much attention to his daughters' education and empowering them did not go down well with some of his colleagues.

Furthermore, the congregation at Apostolic Faith church (vapostori vekwaMarange) frowned upon the way Uncle Walter was raising us. Uncle Walter and his family were members of the Apostolic Faith Church at that time. The church did not believe in educating and empowering women, and Uncle Walter was doing the opposite. In the Apostolic Faith Church, females were only allowed to get educated up to 7th grade and then have an arranged marriage. Women did not have the same rights as men.

One Saturday morning Uncle Walter and family went to church and the whole service was about him, "...fathers who do not follow the laws of the church" was the theme of the sermon. The following week, it was the same thing. It became apparent, some of his work colleagues and subordinates had gone to tell the church leaders about how Uncle Walter treated his daughters. In retaliation, he stopped going to that church. My uncle believed his children male or female, were his priority above everything else. He did not argue with anyone; he did not cause a scene but decided to honor his beliefs and choices. He never set foot in that church again.

Later, as life progressed Judith shared a story with me. One day Uncle Walter came home and told her that he had found her a husband. With confusion on her face, she looked at her mum wondering what was going on since her father had left the Apostolic Faith Church. After a long pause, Uncle Walter said to her, "The husband I have found for you is called a college education. If you keep that husband, he will lead you to getting a college certificate; he will love you forever, look after you, never leave you, feed you and provide for all your needs."

Before long Judith realized Uncle Walter was speaking metaphorically. He was letting her know he had secured a place for her into college and he was willing to support her with whatever she needed to achieve her advanced education. Judith later grew up to become a Lab technician, and to this day she remembers her dad with so much fondness.

Uncle Walter was a very quiet man; he knew each one of us very well and focused on developing our area of strength. My brother, also told me how he used to take them fishing and approached them separately as they were fishing and talked to them about areas which needed to improve such as school subjects, career, behavior, and character. So, he made it a point to give each child undivided attention. He was also a great problem solver; I do miss him.

With the few examples I have shared of the men who played a pivotal role in my life, I wish we celebrated men more and recognize their role in building our community. Let 's give credit where it's due. The more we share these stories, the more other women and men realize that we are supposed to co-exist and fulfill our purpose. Some readers will remember that I had shared my story, about how I ran away from home when I was 17 years old to avoid becoming a child bride. I believe, I managed to take such a bold step because my father had already shaped my character during the early years. He taught, me that I had rights, I could make my own decisions, and I had a choice to aspire to do great things. Even though I was a female, he taught me to believe I was just as important as anyone else.

So, to respond to my friend Vikki's question, why I choose not to stay in an abusive relationship, it's because I believe it is unacceptable to be part of what does not feel natural, to me. My father taught me through his actions that a man is always to show love and affection, to always cherish and care for the family. He showed me unconditional love, and as a result, I believe I deserve always to be cherished.

I will leave you with these three quotes on self-worth:

"Know your worth, if it costs you your peace, it's too expensive." ~ Unknown

"Self-love, Self-respect, and self-worth…there is a reason they all start with 'self.' You cannot find them in anyone else." ~ Unknown

"If you want to improve your self-worth, stop giving other people the calculator." Tim Fargo

My question to you is, Do You Know Your Worth?

Monica Kunzekweguta

Monica Kunzekweguta was born and raised in Zimbabwe. She moved to the United Kingdom in 1994 and lived there for twenty-one years before moving to Canada where she now lives. Monica is a multiple best-selling International Author and compiler. She is a Certified Life Coach, Speaker, and publisher. Monica uses the opportunity to apply her coaching skills to help people transform as they open-up, and blossom through sharing their life experiences to help others. She discovered the power of storytelling and loves to share empowering stories with the world.

A Sociology graduate, Monica gained a lot of experience dealing with life's challenges in the UK, where She worked as a manager in the Mental Health sector for over 15 years. Her resume includes several self-development and leadership Programs.

Monica is Project Founder of Inspiration for Kids International, a charity which provides library books to children living in rural Zimbabwe. She enjoys traveling, reading, watching documentaries, and walking.

Connect with Monica

https://www.linkedin.com/monicakunzekweguta

https://www.silentstrengthbook.com

Facebook: Monica Kunzekweguta

Rejection: Like Earth to Rain

By Damilola Jonathan Oladeji

When I was a little boy, rain meant a lot of things to me. Most importantly it was time to throw caution to the wind and go run outside to play!

The rain reminds me vaguely of a Yoruba incantation; it says, "The earth has never learned how to reject the rain, may I will be like the rain." I remember some things I felt a few years back. It was raining right then as I had these thoughts. I can still imagine the raindrops falling to earth, and the earth receiving without hesitation.

Imagine the sound of rain on the roof and water rolling off on to the ground and the earth having no choice than to accept these streams of joy. We all want to be irresistible. To be indomitable at our worktables, pushing out our demands to the universe and getting an ovation. We want to be influential innovators, intellectuals acknowledged and accepted by the world.

At this point, you probably realize also that that's not going to happen.

You are probably sitting on a thousand stacks of rejection emails. A dozen girls who don't like you. A thousand job applications that are so sorry they won't be taking you this time.

You might even be tempted to stop trying stuff. I have sometimes imagined that someone in these offices I apply to is probably someone that knows me on social media and doesn't like me. Maybe God is testing me!! Rejection makes you paranoid; please don't do that to yourself!

All these crazy thoughts come to mind, but eventually, I think rejection is healthy. In fact, you'd never understand words like persistence, resilience, consistency, and discipline if there was no rejection. If every time, all you got was a "YES!", you'd be such a slob.

I see you bragging about how confident you are, how great you have become and all that effortlessness you put into being the best. Give a little credit to rejection. Understand that you would have been none of that without some "NO!" here and there.

What you forget to tell us is that rejection has whooped you so hard that you'd sweat and keep, late nights, to perfect your act. Yea, I know, it's not easy to sweat at night.

But, that's what rejection does to you.

Remember that little kid you know. The one who always gets his sweets, and never has to tie his shoe. Remember how they'd throw tantrums for the most stupid things. What if, every adult grew up with a habit of throwing tantrums? Just imagine! WOW! The thought of a world filled with tantrum throwing adults scares me.

At least, now we know one good thing rejection has done for the world.

So, while you curse out that editor, and grind your teeth in protest, give some credit to this good old rejection. It's part of what saves our planet.

I realize now that I have grown. There's a lot of things keeping me indoors but most importantly, rejection. I am no longer that little boy who enjoyed the cold wind and splashing of raindrops on my naked skin. I can't always expect the world to align for me as it did when all I wanted was food and a place to sleep.

There's a story in the Bible where Jesus exhorts everyone to be like the little child. How exactly does an adult become like a child in this evil world filled with people who are always so eager to smash your expectations?

Like the rain, children keep falling and running, placing their faith out there that someone will catch them. And like the earth, they accept the world around them without fear. The faith of a child is unchecked and unfettered. He runs with arms stretched and even if you reject him, he will try again. For a while, I stopped being that child.

I became thankful for the rain for a different reason; it made me feel like the world would stop for a bit. I still like that sometimes anyways that I would stop being overwhelmed by the rejections I face every day as an adult.

Now I pray for the rain for a different reason entirely.

I am older now, and the pleasure I have from the rain is different. It feels more like I want it to shield me from the world. I secretly pray every day for the world to stand still for a moment and give me time to breathe.

The only time this prayer is answered is when it rains. I am somehow happy that everyone else would also get to stop whatever they are doing. Nothing else does this much for me.

What changed about me? Why did I switch from that boy who could care less whether it rained, or it shined? The world was my playground; it didn't matter if a flood was drowning people somewhere in Haiti.

Why are you suddenly happy that you cannot go out even if you wanted to? It's not like we don't have so many places to go. Rejection puts us in check.

As a child, rain was my destination. All I wanted was to go out to play. Now if I step out, it's for reasons; meetings, social outings, appointments, deadlines and so on. I have hopes and expectations, and they scare me.

"Going out" has become work for me. The more meaningful my life has become, the more responsible for the time that I have become, the more fearful I am of going out. Now I am so aware of the passing of time.

This is scary. Every time I receive another rejection email, I realize how much time I have lost while waiting. Every waking day is filled with plans and expectations. This frightening reality murders the child in me, hacking him to death. I used to think this is terrible. The child in me, dying off.

"This meeting must be successful, that pitch must win, I must get a new job; this interview must work." I continuously run on a clock, and there's no time to stop and appreciate the moments I am in. Now going out is not an interaction with nature; it's not about the cold sensation of raindrops or the splashing of water. I no longer appreciate the beauty of moments, because everything now makes sense!

Going out now involves me bracing myself for a lot of rejection. This reality scared me for a long time. The more intelligent I have become, the more fearful I have become. Is ignorance not bliss as they say? Maybe it is.

A friend once asked me to write about being rejected. I have come to realize and believe that rejection is the one most potent forces that a lot of us do not understand.

In our search for love and acceptance, we are tied to this fear that we will be rejected. This leaves us perpetually missing out on all that's good about relationships.

Finding love is one of the hardest parts of life. It's harder than finding a job. It's very easy to be a sexual rabbit, humping everything in sight. The hard part is getting someone to look at all your brokenness, eccentricity and accept you. Nowadays you just need to announce that you are horny and there would be someone within the area to service your needs. Sex has become so cheap, love is not.

When it comes to deep, meaningful relationships, a lot of us have gradually grown to dread them because we are too afraid that we will be rejected.

If I have learned anything, it's the art of accepting rejection. What an Irony! Everyone must learn how to appreciate rejection for the value it brings to our lives. Rejection shows you how to lower your expectations, develop a mental shock absorbent and be less entitled to things.

My policy used to be this, "I don't go around making a random selection. If I ask a girl out, it's because I have intentions of getting serious with her."

I have always been a serious and determined child. My intentions and plans have been so central to my every step, that I suffered a lot of heartbreaks. I somehow believed that having good intentions should earn me acceptance. This feeling of entitlement only led to pain and anger.

Let me tell you about job applications and scholarship applications. My approach changed rapidly in recent years. The moment I realized rejection had nothing to do with me, my qualification or my face, I started to change again.

While I was searching for admissions, I got admissions to more than 4 U.K. and international Universities, even though I applied to probably three times that number.

While I was searching for jobs, I applied to so many job openings, even the ones I knew; I would never attend the interview for. I applied for sales clerk jobs, admin officer, polytechnic technical assistant or whatever name they called that position. I applied to several places but then only one or two replied. Only a small number turned into anything good. I received so many rejection emails.

The same thing was happening in my love life. There are many women but only a few will like you enough to accept your advances. There are many men; only a few will think you are a queen.

When you are rejected, carry your bag and baggage, move to the next street and make another application. You will be rejected so many times before you get accepted. Don't expect anybody to be kind about their rejection letter. After all, when companies manage to send a rejection letter, they are not paid to consider your feelings while writing that letter. People will reject you without remorse.

I know, it's always painful to be rejected, but it's just the way life is. It's one of those things designed to push you out of the bubble babies come wrapped in. It's like losing your first tooth or taking your first step. It's an initiation into your identity. Rejection sheds off all the things you think you should be and leaves only who you really are.

I believe strongly that the most exceptional people emerged from a place of being denied options. When you have been rejected so much, you must create your own success. Sometimes, you need to tell yourself, "I have no other choice than to succeed." It's not like anyone else out there wants you anyways. Rejection teaches you to stand by YOU. Be your own number one cheerleader and be loyal to the person you have no choice than to be.

Trust me, a lot of people will not understand you and where you are emerging from, but this is precisely the product of rejection. It strengthens you and gives you unique ideas that stand out.

Eventually, you have become rain, irresistible. The very people who rejected you, would look for you and work with you. The reason this would happen is not so that you can gloat. It's just to let you understand how important it is for you to accept yourself first.

You see all those people who got what you think you didn't get? They also are still on their own journey with rejection. No one misses, out on this class. It's a compulsory one. It's one of those lessons you never stop learning because when you stop learning, you'd be back in that bad place being the spoiled celebrity who cannot be polite to the bartender. You practically lose your humanity, the moment you decide to graduate from the school of rejection.

As more people rejected me, I started to accept myself even more. I embraced my work and gave myself standing ovations. It turns out I am a pretty good writer and that I can actually survive on my own in a foreign country. While I was still in that space where I wanted to be accepted, I had untapped ideas, energy, and capacity. They started to find their way to the surface as I recognized the need to chart a path for myself. Like a child, I now give myself the choice to try again and the ability to applaud myself for every single win.

Damilola Jonathan Oladeji

Damilola Jonathan Oladeji is an author. His story Grey Wine is a fictional chronicle of life as a clergy's child. His work has been on various platforms across the web. He is a research fellow and mentor to a writing community. He loves to tell stories that serve as catalysts for change and growth. In his book "Bloody Ideologies" he gives the reader a chance to question with eyes wide open. He is deliberate in his work and has found a constant passion for storytelling.

Connect with Jonathan:

cfwriterz.com

jonathanoladeji.com

Make It Happen Change Your Life

By Marcela Kyngesburye

When I need inspiration, I think about reading stories of personal transformation. As a teacher, I really enjoy witnessing the profound impact that learning about them has on all of us. At every level, we all have our unique stories of transformation. We are in the midst of them. Under anxiety, pain, stress, blindness, "you name it," we struggle, daily to be present, non-judgmental and at ease with ourselves and others.

Today after many years, I could not be happier facilitating healing in people. I feel like taking before and after pictures every time, for it is not a lie that the eyes are windows of the soul. Being able to share from the heart, to be vulnerable, to be listened to, with kindness, all of these are rare opportunities we encounter in our day to day relationships. One of my favorite practices to do every day is to meet and connect with people where they are and to help them see all the possibilities available to them. To be present during those magical moments of allowance, when the spaces open up, and there are opportunities to experience the unimaginable, this is a priceless gift. The smiles that come from the heart filling the whole being with joy is a passion of mine.

Getting clarity to be free of limitations, energized, revitalized and able to enjoy what comes in life with ease, that is my primary motivation. It all started almost 15 years ago.

Soon after graduating as a Chemical Engineer, I was working for the company of my dreams, making the money I needed to feel happy, wealthy and successful. I had my dream apartment, my loving pets Sophie and Hugh, two adorable cats, I was enjoying being in a steady relationship and surrounded by supportive and caring coworkers that soon became friends and family. I was so proud of myself.

Everything was going just right. I was working shifts; the night shift was from 10 pm to 6 am, the morning one from 6 am to 2 pm and then the evening one from 2 pm to 10 pm. My schedule changed from night to morning, to evening, every six days. I had become so good at my job that I had "earned," or so I thought, the title of Substitute. This meant that I could cover a shift for anyone at the last minute. So, I would be notified daily what would be my shift. The feeling of satisfaction blinded me; I did not consider how the effects this would bring to my body. I am sure you can already imagine what came as a result of that!

Well, you are right. A chain of events changed my life completely. After almost two years of basically not having a natural rhythm in my sleep and eating habits, my body one day started bleeding. I thought it was my period, so at first, I did not worry too much but then it was nonstop and in quantities that I had never experienced before. You can imagine how scared I was! I was living in a very small town and had to drive myself to the doctor in the closest city, in absolute confusion. It took me almost three hours and a half, maybe more, in the weakest physical state. Remember these were not really internet or GPS times, definitely not in my country, Mexico.

I was desperately looking for streets going from one to the other, trying to find an available physician, a phone, a yellow pages' book from that city, or someone who would take walk-ins. Finally, I found one! I do not even recall his name, or the address or anything around it but I can still see myself sitting at his office in front of his desk, anxious to hear that whatever I had was going to be fixed, yes fixed, and as soon as possible just like a machine. Of course, I had to go back and get to work right away. There was no time to be sick! I was needed; I had to be there.

After hours of waiting, the diagnosis was severe anemia, to which I thought "Oh...well, ok, now that we know, let's keep on going, what medicines do I need to take?" And then the REAL news came when the doctor said: "... some signs indicate the possible presence of Precancerous Cells in your body."

BIG TIME SILENCE

"...more studies will be needed; you will need to go to Mexico City to find a doctor who can help you." Mexico City? That was at least eight hours away. He kept going, "We need to have a full panorama of what is happening, and we need to know how it is going to be treated."

It was SHOCKING!

I was for sure not expecting THAT one!

Still very weak, I drove myself back home. With the news that was generating all kinds of thoughts and feelings, the strongest being uncertainty, frustration, loneliness, helplessness, not knowing what to think of the future, not sure of how I was to react towards that which was coming next, blaming myself, my work, others, for what was happening to me. I am telling you of my fall, into a pit, a deep dark black pit, which was in its initial stage.

To make a long story short, in a couple of weeks the decisions I made based on fear and filled with uncertainty made me spiral down and become jobless, apartment-less, pet-less, boyfriend-less, you name it! Everything happened at once.

All the things I had worked for, dreamed of, accomplished, searched for, crashed really quickly and took me into a hopeless land of deep depression!

It was maybe a whole year, literally, in a litter box. I took on the responsibility of caring for a couple of ferrets. They kept me connected emotionally to a past that had vanished and that I was still longing for. Keeping me attached to thoughts and emotions that constantly caused me more suffering. These little pets were not litter trained, so you can imagine the consequences of a whole week, of them playing around in a small apartment. I spent every Saturday cleaning up. Every time it was a Herculean task. It certainly took all the energy I had gathered by sleeping my way through the week or maybe was it the other way around and was I recovering from the task throughout the week?

You may be asking yourself now "What happened with the illness? How was it treated?" Well, I did go to the doctor in Mexico, City, after all, I had moved back to my mom's, and it was only two hours away. Even though I did not want to face it, I had no excuse. I went there for a series of tests and sessions. It was all very new. The doctor was young and figuring it out too. What could I do? Simply TRUST. He was the only choice, he was the EXPERT, and he was the one adventuring into doing this back then. I remember him using a technology he didn't know was going to work or not, and he just did what he thought best. It was very stressful to wait without knowing what that truly meant. For me, it was life, present, future. The decision was made. It was going to be an outpatient surgery, using cryotherapy, a liquid nitrogen procedure that freezes cells. I had worked with it in college. I never thought it would once become a healing agent for my body. Was I Afraid? Definitely. The day came, and after all, was done, I was utterly exhausted. The doctor said that the surgery was going to have the same effects as any other. He was right. I had to rest and recover. I realized that I was going to need more than physical healing.

Anyways, in that mindset, without knowing what was going to come, without striving because there was no physical strength left, everything started to shut down, including my emotional, and mental bodies. I am eternally grateful to my mom, who was there for me the whole time, all the way, without asking anything, giving me her unconditional pure love, and just unwavering support from the heart. I was living with almost no energy, had no money, and no clue about how I was going to be generating it anytime soon. And in a way I was getting used to this way of feeling, accepting being beaten down, thinking it was a place where I was going to stay forever. There was no hope for a different way of living. I was far away from any clue or inspiration whatsoever, or even the will to do so.

In my search for deep understanding, I joined my grandma's Christian community. I had always been attracted to the generosity, gratitude, and spirituality that could be felt in those communities. I desperately needed support and became a fervent member. It was not difficult for me to do so. I had been part of different Christian communities in the past. When I was younger, I had started on a path towards becoming a missionary and had developed a deep relationship with the spiritual world. As I grew older and went to college, I left behind those thoughts and practices and found myself coming back thirsty for the warmth and love; I needed that connection desperately.

A day came when there was this big campaign for organ donation. I said, "Yeah let's do it!" I was so into it and was telling everybody. Literally shouting it to the four winds, "When I die, please, remember to donate my organs." Until I came to my very good friend's presence and she said, "What?" I shared with her that we were in this amazing campaign and were so sure about this, that I was not only happy about doing it but also encouraging others to do so. I can still remember the look on her face. She took me aside and said, "Just stop saying that now, please, I will explain later."

Indeed, once we got to her house and for many more days to come, she taught me what the wisdom of the Tibetans had shared about death. Specifically, what happens at the moment of death followed by the three days after. I was so connected with what I was listening to; I felt mesmerized by the teachings. I knew they resonated with my heart. That was the last time I talked about donating my organs. I definitely stopped encouraging others. My shouting started being "Please, leave my body alone, do not touch it!" I had to do a lot of this to counteract my previous campaign.

At the church, I did not feel the same way either. "What was going to happen next?" I asked myself. A polarity arose while attending the Christian services. As much as a former lifesaver, I now was asking a lot of questions which opened my awareness. I was listening to ideas that didn't belong to me, and more so felt imposed. I had to find new ways to relate and embrace ancient wisdom.

New possibilities showed up. I came back to my friend's house, and she also taught me Qigong, a holistic system of coordinated body posture and movement, breathing, and meditation used for the purposes of health, spirituality, and martial arts training. Qigong has been one of the most powerful gifts I have ever received. Let me show you why? Throughout that whole year, I was telling myself over and over what a failure I was until I drained my brain. I remember sleeping my way through life. I was feeling terribly lonely, with no energy.

It was then that I took the firm resolution to practice Qigong DAILY without exception for a full year. I committed myself that I would do it, with no excuses! Nothing was going to stop me from doing it! Every single day, I knew within myself that failing yet again was not an option. It was like getting charged up, and I told myself that if I missed ONE single day, everything I had GAINED was going to be ERASED and I would have to start from ZERO. That was freaking scary. That made me stay consistent.

As a result of this resolution, I could feel sensations in my body that were not there before. I had more vitality, and this allowed me to connect with people again, with friends and neighbors. I started using my magic again, that light inside of me, that had been suppressed for so long. The time had come; I was able to acknowledge myself again. Little by little, I created low key jobs that would allow me space to keep recovering. During that period, I found that energy was not just in the machines or in chemical reactions. I looked at it for the first time in the air, in fruits and vegetables, in nature, and in me.

I met a family that invited me over to their house. They had a little kid. I was not fond of little kids at the time, I didn't have the energy for them, and yet there I was. Looking back now I recognize how I had allowed myself to be dead inside while being alive. I found ways to spend more and more time with that special three-year-old girl. Her smiles, her love, her tenderness brought me back to life. This unique relationship helped me get back to living on the inside. I started working with crystals and creating pieces of jewelry, that had both beauty and healing properties. It was a brand designed by her mom which was wholly thought of as a path to healing through beauty.

Then I learned from her also a healing technique called Pranic Healing. I went from having no ENERGY to recognizing its qualities, exploring its levels in different objects, measuring its size, and just being curious about it in every possible way. I began to study its behavior in different situations. I resolved to go deeper, do everything to understand it better. Went to classes, workshops, retreats, practiced what I learned, I needed to know how energy moved in our bodies. I studied how to use it to HEAL. I was studying how to use crystals, how energy worked, how to use colors, how to protect myself and others and how to help with addictions and other ailments (like my deep depression) using Pranic Psychotherapy. Little did I know that a full year of experiencing and noticing the sensations present in my body, emotions, and thoughts, and letting them speak to me, was going to open so many doors.

That was just the beginning of a journey that would lead to so many imminent, joyful transformations. My life changed the minute I realized the importance of observing my body, its energy, and vitality. Pausing, being aware of my breath, meditating, the effects of SIMPLE movements, made such a difference! That awareness was tremendous; staying healthy became a priority. I was amazed at the direct consequences that my thoughts and emotions also had on my physical body. So many "aha" moments! Clearing repeated patterns, such as "I am not good enough," and "I do not deserve," became a habit, as well as identifying beliefs that were not mine, oh what a release! I started nurturing my body with delicious food, with exercise, my emotions with love and gratitude, my thoughts with meditation and universal wisdom.

My energy was back; I was no longer in survival mode, trying to get everything done, feeling exhausted, or stressed. All of that was replaced! I was waking up with a purpose, with a passion. I said goodbye to the confusion, to the untidiness, I was making decisions with clarity and holding myself to high standards. Life became worth living. Although unwanted thoughts or emotions would appear again, I knew now how to listen to them, how to notice what to do in their presence. Uncertainty wasn't any more a paralyzing force. Instead, it brought me infinite possibilities. The results were amazing. I found myself going through the changes with a big smile coming straight from my heart and filling my whole body with a great sense of ease.

I reinvented myself and started teaching others how to do the same: I NOW watch how their new levels of awareness create transformation in many aspects of their lives too! I have since committed to dedicating the rest of my professional life to helping others going through an identity renewal, to reconnect with their truth, with their life purpose and mainly with their deepest desires of the heart.

Since then, I've worked with private clients and have lived my dream of sharing my gifts with others. I have created "Bliss in all the Right Places: Reinvent Yourself in 90 days", a series of 9 important inner and outer steps to transformation for every person who finds themselves ready to reinvent themselves in record time.

This story of transformation started a series of events that I would have never imagined. From a profound feeling of helplessness, thinking that there was no sense in finding a purpose, and sunk in absolute depression, to a rising through the recognition of the senses, the identification of the realms of energy healing, of relaxed awareness, to enthusiasm for life. I learned to be open, to start living without expectations, allowing guidance and letting go of what I do not need. Especially all those negative thoughts and emotions, all those limiting beliefs stopping me from moving forward. Allowing for Trust and Faith to be my companions, a special kind of ease was in me and still is. Now I turn back and speak to my younger self with a lot of love, compassion, kindness, and tenderness.

It fills me with joy to open my eyes to a time in my life in which I see the results of all those insights. I can see how growing older allows for life events to be less dramatic, less attached. That is why I want to keep teaching, how you can MAKE IT HAPPEN and Change Your LIFE!

I hope this chapter, inspires you to find what brought you to this moment, to live with ease with what is. To observe where you are today or maybe better, to the place where you are open to all your inner abilities and recognizing that they are ready to be expressed in the world. You are unique; you are a gift to others! The time to bring out the best, shiniest version of YOU is NOW!!!

Light and Love,

Marcela Kyngesburye

Marcela is a Transformational Coach, passionate about using the wisdom of the body, the emotions, the thoughts, and the present moment awareness, to bring JOY to life!

She has worked with clients to discover their limiting beliefs, recurring patterns, and has helped them to create new mindsets that allow them to achieve a lifetime of joy, ease, and abundance.

Before becoming a Transformational coach, Marcela was a Chemical Engineer who worked for Nestlé, Praxair and enjoyed the complexity of the automotive industry. She trained and worked as a Waldorf Teacher which deepened her understanding of human development. She has created a unique way to bring to life and share with others the benefits of the energy healing modalities she has studied and practiced for over 15 years.

She continues to teach Mindfulness to teachers, so they are aware of the impact they have on the social, emotional, psychological and environmental aspects of their students.

Born and raised in Mexico, she now resides in the U.S. She enjoys reading, biking and most of all spending time with her husband!

To connect with Marcela:

info@marcelacoaching.com

http://www.marcelakyngesburye.com

https://www.facebook.com/MarcelaKyngesburye/

Change Your Thoughts Change Your Life
Part 1

By Joyce Hativagone Damiso

It was two hours since the beginning of my shift, and I noticed that Vera had not come to my office to give me a report on the patients. Every day after the outgoing nurse left, Vera, a nursing assistant in her thirties would come to the office to give me her version of what transpired in the previous shift. She didn't have to, but she loved to talk. I listened. I had no choice. Although I preferred an interactive conversation, she made it almost impossible. I stopped fighting her over it. That was our routine. So, this was very unusual for her. From where I stood in my office, I studied her body language, and the expression on her face indicated something was going on. It was not like her to sit idle and stare into space. Something was definitely amiss. I decided to find out.

I walked to where she was sitting, pulled a chair and sat across from her. When I asked if everything was okay, instead of answering, she started crying. Tears ran down her cheeks effortlessly. That was one side of her that I had never seen. Seeing her crying like that broke my heart and disturbed me. She did not believe in crying and had very little tolerance of people who cried. She perceived it as a weakness in personality and attention seeking. Even the patients she took care of at the mental health facility knew that Vera would tolerate the adolescents screaming or acting out, but crying was not her thing. She was not a weak person, and there she was crying.

I was stunned, and I sat helplessly not knowing what to do or say. I felt a tremble go through my body. I didn't mean to be intrusive, and I regretted starting and engaging in the conversation. I certainly didn't see that coming. She was my friend, and her unusual behavior concerned me. I wanted to comfort her; put my hand on hers and assure her it would be fine. I couldn't do that because I didn't even know why she was crying and knowing her, I knew she didn't want to be the object of pity. I also didn't know how she would respond, so I sat there and waited. She knew I was a good listener. She had turned me into one, and I hoped she would open up and talk to me sooner than later.

She did, eventually, after about five minutes. When she looked at me, hard pain was evident in her eyes. With a broken voice, the first thing she told me was that I was the fourth person she was sharing her life experience with. I was curious to know what it was she wanted to share with me, but I was also touched!

"There are certain life experiences you just don't talk about," she said between sobs. "Talking about it is like ripping off the bandage on a fresh wound. It doesn't matter how long ago it happened; it still hurts."

I almost told her not to talk about it if it hurt that much, but I had a feeling she wanted to vent, or at least tell me the story. I handed her a tissue, but she didn't use it to wipe away the tears. Instead, she folded it neatly and then used it to wipe the tears falling on the table. Her body was tight, obviously filled with bad memories and experience she was reliving.

The people who knew her story included her mom, her husband, and her counselor and of course the people involved. These perpetrators had abused her sexually, emotionally and done enough damage to ruin and steal her childhood, destroying her self-esteem in the process.

"Some things can never be forgotten no matter how hard you try," Vera said her face still streaked with tears.

She told me that she was abused from the age of five and this continued until she was twelve years old. It stopped when her sister intervened unknowingly when she decided to work from home after childbirth. Her presence at home, taking care of her baby made it hard for the perpetrators to come. As she talked about her ordeal, I gathered at least two men molested her although she would not say how many exactly or who they were.

"It was family that's why it hurts so much. These are people everyone trusted to be around me including me. When they started, I didn't understand what they were doing or why, but I knew it was not right. When I threatened to report them to my mother, or sister, they threatened me too. One of them told me that he would take me into the woods and leave me there to die and that no one would ever find me. I believed him.

One by one they would come at different times, and different days. I don't know if they talked about me between themselves. I know one thing; they never arrived at the same time. They hurt me so bad. I was powerless and didn't have the physical ability to stop them. I didn't know what else to do but for them to stop.

I felt like I was living someone else's life and that things would be different when I grow up. I wanted to grow up so much, so I could be my own person, and nobody would dare touch me without my consent. But the battle has continued. Yes, I am all grown up now; they can't touch me physically but mentally and emotionally; they will always reach me. I sometimes feel those hands creeping over my body." She shrugged.

She was still crying quietly. It was a good thing that it was just her and me in the patient's dayroom at that time. The patients were all in bed sleeping. It would have been difficult to explain what was going on. It was hard enough for me to see her like this. Vera was not an emotional person, and that would have confused them. She was liked and respected by the patients, and that was not someone they knew. I wanted to protect both the patients and Vera. She certainly would not have wanted anyone else to see her in that state not to mention the rumors that would follow.

"I never asked for that kind of attention," she continued. "I don't know why they did that to me. I didn't think I was any different from other kids, but they picked on me. I would look myself in the mirror for hours trying to see if I had some kind of mark or something that made them pick on me, but I didn't see anything." I listened without interrupting, but I could feel the tears starting in my eyes. I tried to blink them away. I couldn't do this, not in front of her.

"I know it's a shock to you," she added. "No one knows of the inner hopelessness that engulfs me except for my husband to some extent. I hide my negative emotions. I can't wear them on the sleeve for the world to see. What are they going to do anyway, sympathize with me? I don't need that."

I nodded slowly. Vera was right but shocked, that was an understatement. I tried not to show it though. I just looked at her speechless. Who would have thought that of her, of all the people? She was a dominant, even-keeled woman who was not easily ruffled, yet she was dealing with so much inner pain, and still going on with her business as if all was well. I felt my mouth open, but no words came. Nobody deserved to be abused; sexually, emotionally or physically, child or adult.

"For the longest time, I thought it was my fault, that I had done something wrong. I wanted to tell my sister so badly, but I didn't know how to express myself. So, to get attention, I started acting out, both at home and school. I hated my life; I hated my school. I was moody and rebellious. I got into trouble a lot. I changed, but not for the better. I didn't particularly have friends. I was always so sad. So, they left me alone, and I was okay with it.

I didn't get the support I wanted from my family. Instead, I got punished or whipped for acting out. I didn't know what else to do. I didn't understand why my family could not protect me. I was hurting and so alone. I cried so hard at the grand injustice of it all."

She went on to tell me how she tried unsuccessfully to commit suicide three times.

"After the third attempt, I vowed I would never try again. It was so unfortunate I didn't have the gun; it might have worked who knows. My husband knew better than to keep one in the house. He has a collection that he keeps at his parents' house. I won't try again that's for certain. I don't want permanent physical or brain damage because of failed attempts. The third time was not a good experience, and that was my turning point. I almost died, but I believe God stopped it from happening for a reason. I know about His love, and the plan He has for me has kept me going. I believe I have a purpose; to help the kids like the ones in our care who are dealing with similar situations. That is why I took this job. I have dedicated my life to working with them, and the Holy Spirit is directing and guiding me; otherwise I wouldn't be able to do it. I see so much of me in them; the pain, the hopelessness, helplessness, and the anger. It's terrifying. I try to encourage them to be strong. I listen to them when they talk. I like them to know that we care, and we are here for them, the way no one was there for me. Regardless of what happened, they still have a life to live, and my favorite quote to them is, 'change your thoughts, change your life.' I know it's easier said than done, but I want them to think differently and not focus on what happened to them. I encourage them to have a vision of their future, to write down their goals and work towards achieving them.

She talked about those moments when she has flashbacks, and then acute depression sets in.

"I live in bondage of depression. I sometimes get into terrible depression. I start with this feeling of sadness deep in my stomach. I don't fight it; I go with the emotions. I give myself time and space for solitude, and I descend into this darkness. I don't eat or drink. I don't leave my bed. I remember everything they did to me. It's painful, this is the worst part, and it lasts for at least a few days. It could be more if I let it, but after so many days, I drag myself out of bed, put a smile on my face and continue with my life. I will be dying inside though. During that time my husband gives me space and leaves me alone. I know it's a lot for him, but he knew what he was getting into when he married me. He knows how much I hate it, but it is what it is.

I don't take medication," she said before I asked her. "I tried. They don't work for me, and I don't like to be dependent on them either. For the most part, I am okay. It hits me every once in a while. The triggers are the smell, colors or a word, and just anything sets it off. It's always different."

She had stopped crying then. "I think I am healing some or I am getting better at blocking it." She laughed with disdain.

As I sat there listening, some things were beginning to make sense about her. She was a hard-working lady, an energy doer. Every day she would come to work early so she would clean the unit, wipe down surfaces and organize stuff. She was obsessed with cleanliness and orderliness a habit she had developed during her ordeal.

"Cleanliness was one thing I started getting obsessed about," she explained. "I would scrub myself after every encounter, trying to wipe away any trace of them. First, it was just my body, and then it was everything around me. I just wanted cleanliness and organization in everything. I wasn't born with the obsessive-compulsive disorder. It developed. It also kept me busy, taking my mind off things."

The excessive talking was one of her coping skills that her therapist had recommended. She would talk endlessly about anything. She was a very intelligent woman and although now and then I would ask for a bit of silence or play gospel music. It never worked. We had a conversation about everyday life, life experiences, her experience and she did most of the talking which made me listen without really intending to. She knew how to make it engaging and before I knew it she had my attention without me realizing it. I liked it that we could talk about anything which was a sign of our good connection.

I then asked about the husband. I had met him twice when he came to pick her up from work. He seemed fine in both character and looks.

"I met Luke in college. I didn't want anything to do with men after my experience with those perpetrators. When I met my husband things changed. I don't know how but he managed to crack through this impenetrable wall I had built around me to avoid getting close to anyone, especially men. He was persistent and would not leave me alone. Maybe I didn't want him to. I liked him. He was at that time the only person closest to me then. I had distanced myself from my family. So, I told him about my ordeal, so he would know what he was getting into if he chose to stay. I honestly expected him to run the other way, but instead, he wanted to help me. He suggested I see a counselor. I never wanted to before, but he insisted, and I did. The counselor then advised me to tell my mom everything. I was reluctant at first. I was twenty-two then, and that was ten years ago when it happened. I agreed because we all thought it would help me heal. How wrong we were."

She paused, shook her head before she continued.

"Mom told me she kind of suspected it. She was sorry she did nothing about it. Sorry! Can you believe that? You suspect something like that is happening to your five, six, seven, eight, or twelve-year-old child and you don't do anything about it. She could at least have asked me. At the time I did not know whether to scream at her or just walk out of her house. I did neither."

"She's a jerk, "I said defensively, hearing that judging tone in my voice.

She laughed lightly, "My mother didn't raise me. My eldest sister did, but we lived next door to each other. She was sick after my birth and my sister offered to take care of me since I was a baby. My sister is my mom in every sense of the word." She took a deep breath before she continued.

"She then called the men in question one by one and asked them to apologize to me. What they offered wasn't even an apology and whatever it was didn't make me feel any better. I don't think they were sincere either. I think they were more embarrassed than sorry. Anything coming from them said or unsaid would not make any difference. They had done their damage, and no amount of apologizing would change that. I hated seeing them again. Since mom had insisted, and I was the one who had gone to her, I had to bear with it. Them being family made it difficult for mama to do anything since it had happened a long time ago. That was her explanation. And it would cause a lot of commotion in the family.

The truth is, I did not expect anything from those abusers, but I did expect something from my mom. I don't know what exactly it was I expected from her, but I know one thing, I didn't get it. I didn't get anything. To her, it was a done deal. The perpetrators had apologized, and I was expected to accept the apology and put a closure to the whole thing, put everything behind me, move on with my life and never talk about it ever again to anyone. She didn't ask me how I felt, or if I was okay with what she did. That was a blow to me, and I have never looked at her the same way. The wall between us only thickened." I felt my stomach tighten.

I wanted very much to ask her why she didn't talk to her sister, but maybe the husband was one of the perpetrators. She told me she was closer to her than she was to her mom. As if she read my mind, she said, "I was afraid to tell anyone about it because of the threats, and I prayed my sister would figure it out. She's a voice of reason and doesn't miss much, but not with me. Apparently she missed it all." I looked at her troubled face.

Her forehead cricked into a frown. "My sister might have raised me, but I still have a mother. I sometimes think she didn't care because we didn't have that bond. It was never my choice not to live with my mother. In my own way I loved her and looked up to her.

"I have forgiven them though," she said.

"Forgiven who?" I asked. She gave me you-know-who-I-am-talking-about look.

Of course I did. I shook my head in disbelief. "You did what?" I asked trying to take the bitterness out of my voice.

"I had to for me. I gave them the benefit of the doubt. If they knew better, they might have behaved differently. I can't change anything now, and if I don't let go, I may end up doing something about it, like opening a can of worms which would lead to too many people being hurt and families breaking up without a doubt. I can't live with myself hurting innocent people like that. Majority of them are innocent whether we like it or not. I can't make the whole family pay for the sins of one person. Also, as Christians; we are reminded to forgive those who offend us so that we can be forgiven. I know it sounds ridiculous, but it is what it is."

She just shrugged her shoulders, and continued, "Do you know how people who have been hurt like to hurt others, or people who have been taken advantage of, like to do that to someone else. It becomes a vicious circle. I have seen that too often, and I don't want to be that person. I have to let go so I can move on."

I don't think I will ever understand how she could ever forgive them, but that was her call. She said she didn't want that responsibility of breaking up families. All she wanted was to heal and move on with her life. I didn't think she was doing an excellent job of it though. If she was improving, then why was she on and off in depression? I believe she was still in a lot of pain.

"I know you have to decide the forgiving part yourself, but…." I shook my head in disbelief. But I knew it was churlish to argue with her. She had lived it, experienced it, and above all, it was her decision.

"The darkness in my life is real, and I will forever be seeking the light. I have a long way to go before my wounds heal if they ever will. I take it one day at a time. This job helps me a lot since some of these kids have been victims like me; I understand their pain. I know what they are going through. I am here to encourage them and let them know there is life ahead of them. This is my God-given assignment, and I mean to do it to the end. I can't get through to everyone, but if I make a difference to that one kid, that's all that matters to me."

Admittedly Vera was good at her job. She was more than capable. She had the friendly face and kids warmed to her easily. They adored and felt safe around her. She was also strict with them and had some expectations from them. Most of the patients however preferred to be on her right side and they complied.

She interacted with them, encouraged them; I wish I had a way with words as she did. I believe God was using her to touch these young people's lives who came to our facility for various reasons mostly depression, self-harming and suicidal thoughts. Those patients, mostly adolescents were victims of sexual abuse. I don't know how she did it though considering what she had been through; dealing with all the adolescents issues and not focus on her past which was so similar to her own experiences.

Vera still looked sad but had stopped crying. One of the girls must have had a nightmare and was screaming. She went to check on her. I went back to the office. I realized we had been talking for more than an hour. I knew it was not easy for her to open up to me, but I am glad she had and hoped I was able to provide some empathy and shoulder for her to lean on. When she came back from the patient's room, she gave me a thumbs-up that the girl was okay. She sat down and bowed her head. I think she was praying.

As soon as I sat on my desk, tears came tearing at my heart. It's one thing when you deal with a patient, but when it's someone close to you, it is a different story.

Her sad story was packed with a lot of lessons. It brought instant transformation into my way of thinking about my job. I began to look at the patients and try to understand the ordeal they had gone through which made them end up in our care. Everyone's story was different, but I had never really looked at them as anything but patients. I had never asked any one of them to share their whole story with me. All I knew was the short version which we got on admission which was in the chart and on file. Of course, the therapists did a more detailed in-depth treatment plan, but as part of the team, we had a job to do too. Not to put out the fire when they acted out. I know some of them were more than willing to share their experience, maybe for sympathy or empathy or perhaps just to offload their burdened hearts. I had intentionally distanced myself from knowing their real issues for fear of being emotionally involved. I had seen some people get torn at heart and ended up leaving the job or making the wrong decisions. What some of them had gone through was beyond understanding. I asked myself several times, why them? Wat did they do to deserve that kind of treatment.

Generally, the patients were admitted for depression, suicidal thoughts or self-harming because of their experiences. At our facility we counseled, medicated and then released them back into the world, to deal with life. No matter how unfortunate the circumstances were, the victims had to accept what had happened to them, and learn to move on with life hard as it was.

Sometimes they had to live in the same environment they were hurt or stay with the people who didn't do much to protect them. My focus like everyone else was on their behavior when they acted out which was wrong sometimes. We focused on calming them down without really trying to figure out what was going on, or what had triggered the outburst. I decided to become more than just a nurse. It was an opportunity for me too to step up and be there for these young people. I knew I couldn't help all of them, but that one person was a good start. I appreciated Vera more and wanted to learn from her how she got through to these young adults. That was more than just a job. It took a special person to know not only what to say but how and when to say it. That was a calling for Vera, but for me, it was work in progress. I had a lot to learn. Good thing, I was more than ready to. With a good teacher like Vera, I believe I can make that difference. I pray that by sharing this story, I will be helping victims of sexual abuse and stop perpetrators in their tracks.

Joyce Hativagone Damiso

Joyce Hativagone Damiso was born and raised in Harare, Zimbabwe. A graduate of Oklahoma State University, she is a Registered Nurse and has worked in this field for seven years. She started her career in the Health Field where she worked as a carer in the United Kingdom for four years before migrating to the United States of America. An entrepreneur at heart Joyce was also Chief Executive Officer for Raindrops Counselling services from 2014 to May 2018.

Even though Joyce has always loved to write, her career is just beginning as this is her first published story. She is currently working on more short stories and looks forward to publishing her book before the end of the year.

One of her passions is reading mostly Christian and fiction books. She loves traveling which helps her connect with new people.

The Damisos are blessed with two daughters, a son and a grandson and currently live in Oklahoma City.

To connect with Joyce:

tyradrops3@gmail.com

https://www.facebook.com/joycehativagonedamiso

The Power of A Changed Mind Part 2

By Joyce Hativagoni Damiso

After working night shift, I usually average about six to seven hours of sleep a day, but today when I opened my eyes, I had a feeling I had woken up too early. I rolled over in my bed and reached out for my phone on the nightstand; I wanted to look at the time. It was only 11:30 in the morning. I did some math in my head and figured I had slept for only three hours. That wasn't good considering I had to go back to work later that evening. I don't take any sleeping aids, because I have never had to. All I need is a dark, quiet room, and since I am the only one at home at that time, it works well.

I closed my eyes tight and willed for sleep to come, but after thirty minutes or so of tossing and turning I gave up. I reached for the remote control and turned on the television. I grabbed two pillows and slid them under my neck, so I could watch television without sitting upright, just in case I fell asleep. I flipped through the channels not sure what I was looking for. When I was on TBN (the world's largest religious network and America's most watched channel), there was this young female gospel singer I didn't recognize, Prim and Proper, who sang in a rich and melodious voice. I didn't know the song she was singing, but I liked it. I was now glued to the television screen. The young lady sang two more gospel songs and bowed down as she was getting ready to exit the stage. The crowd broke into thunderous applause. She then waved at them, a big smile on her face and walked away. She had given it her all. She had delivered.

Even though I enjoyed the music, at the back of my mind, I was thinking about Vera, my friend from work. She had sent me a message earlier saying she was wasn't in a good place. I knew what that meant. She was depressed, again. I couldn't help but worry about her, maybe that's why I couldn't stay asleep. I had not seen her for a whole week at work. She took some time off, family emergency I was told. I knew better. I didn't try to check on her. I gave her the space that I knew she needed. How I wished I could do something different to help her, but even as a close friend there was only so much, I could do.

Ever since she had shared her life story with me about six months ago, I encouraged her to call me, text me or even come to my house whenever she wanted to talk. We had spoken on the phone several times, exchanged a few messages, and she had been to my house a few times.

Just as I was thinking about Vera waiting for whatever was coming next on television after the advertisements (hopefully another singer), a fifty-something-year-old woman, dressed in a black and white suit and matching shoes stepped on the stage. She introduced herself as Pastor Myranda, from a Pentecostal church in Dallas. I gathered she wasn't going to sing but had a message that she wanted to share with the audience and the whole world at large. She looked polished and congenial. When she started talking, I did not pay much attention to her although I heard everything she said. I was hoping to fall back to sleep.

It was when she mentioned that she was a victim of sexual abuse and wanted to reach out to other victims who had the same experience. As I listened to her, that caught my attention. She said that four men molested her for twelve years. She didn't give any more details, but that was enough. I quivered with righteous indignation. What was the world coming to? What was wrong with these people? I had had enough of these stories, and I was about to turn to another channel, but something about the way she was narrating her story made me stay on that channel.

I figured that for her to be telling her story she must have helped some people heal or that was a process of healing for her to have the courage to talk about it on television without breaking down publicly. Four men? Twelve years, just when you thought you had heard it all. I believe what she had gone through was not too different from what Vera and other women out there had gone through. I was curious to know how she had managed to come out of it. I wanted to listen to her more. I hoped I would learn something from her experience, so I could better understand and help Vera.

Her story sad as it was, had me captivated. She was a lively, energetic speaker and her conversation style was engaging. She used a lot of hand gestures as she walked up and down the podium talking. She was sending her message loud and clear to all the victims of sexual abuse like her, who were out there in the world suffering, hurting, feeling ashamed and blaming themselves for what was done to them. She was good.

Vera needed to listen to her, I thought. I was now really tuned in and wanted to hear the rest of her story. I wrote down her contact details, her name, and website address. I believed it was necessary for her to listen to this from someone who had gone through the same ordeal as her and knows how she had survived it.

"Yes, twelve years of my life they stole from me," the pastor continued. "After I was free, they stole another two years. The two years I spent in depression, going through all kinds of emotions, feeling sorry for myself, the guilt and shame for not having been able to prevent it although I knew at the time, there was nothing I could do. I did think of ending my life a lot, but I didn't have the guts to do it, so I suffered quietly. I prayed to God wondering why He was not answering me. Despite not getting an answer from Him, my faith in Him sustained me. I believed He still could hear me.

Those fourteen years were the hardest part of my life. I kept praying for a miracle that would erase the pain, and memories and make me forget what happened." She paused. Her voice was thick with emotion. I could hear the pain in it.

"I didn't have a past because my past was still my present in every sense of the word. I kept reliving that life even after the abuse was over. I was still a slave to those people. Nothing had managed to erase it, not that I was doing anything towards it. I honestly didn't think there was a way out. I thought I would always live my life in misery. It was as if the whole world knew what had happened to me and even if they did, they didn't stop living, and that hurt.

This was my life, until one day I decided to obey that small voice that had been nagging me for a while, urging me to put the past behind me and move on with my life but had intentionally ignored. I needed to do just that. I had to learn to love myself again and reconnect with the world. It was hard, but what choice did I have.

"Yes," she sighed heavily, "my life had been ruined, but I had to decide how I wanted to live what was left of it. My future, unlike my past, was not tarnished. It was going to be as good as how I wanted it to be. Would I let those men continue to haunt me and steal my life from me? I would never forget what happened much as I wanted to, but at the same time, I wasn't benefiting much from reliving it. Moving forward wasn't an option. I had to do it.

After making that commitment to get my life back, I took the first step of calling my counselor whom I had ignored for a long time. I needed someone to be accountable to, someone to share everything with, I could not walk this road of recovery on my own.

I started working on myself by doing the basic things like taking a shower at least more than once or twice a week, wearing clothes instead of staying in pajamas all day and staying in front of the television, snacking nonstop. It was a lot of work. It was hard work. I reduced my drinking and smoking. That was hard, very hard. I wasn't ready to stop yet, that would come with time. I worked on my eating habits, tried to include some healthy stuff. I started taking walks in the neighborhood. It was a long process, awkward at first but with time I started enjoying the freedom from my self-imposed jail.

Going back to church was another challenge. While I prayed all the time at home, I still missed the fellowship of my local church and the spiritual environment. Just like with everything else, I had to start from somewhere. It was a long time since I had stepped foot in the church. I started by walking past it, checking it out when I went for walks. The next thing I knew I found myself inside it, but I would sit at the back, making sure I was the first one out. I avoided fellowshipping with other people in case they wanted to know more about me or someone recognized me. Before I knew it, the church became my sanctuary. I felt at home, and I thought I belonged. With time I actively got involved in church activities, and by doing so, I made a bunch of Christian friends. I had no idea that one day, week after week, I would stand in front of people, in different churches, talking about my story with the hope of inspiring and encouraging someone.

Now at the age of fifty-two, I am married with children and grandchildren. I always compare my life with that bible story about a crippled man beside the Bethesda pool, who in a desperate situation lay on the mat waiting for someone to come and rescue him. He was in that condition for thirty-eight years until Jesus healed him and told him to pick up his mat and walk. Mine was only fourteen years before Jesus came to my rescue. He healed me. When He said to me through that small voice that I had continuously ignored to pick up my mat and walk, I did just that. I started with baby steps and look at me now. The thing is, once you start you will eventually get somewhere. The important thing is to start.

"I am a survivor of sexual abuse," she continued, her voice filling with emotion. "I was left with scars, that will never go away. For me, they are constant reminders of what was then, not anymore. They are scars, not fresh wounds. It's still hard to look at them, but they don't hurt.

Sometimes even after making progress with the healing, we may find ourselves picking on the wounds that were getting better or removing the scabs. The wound starts to bleed again and guess what, it takes us a few steps back, but we must continue with the process. We cannot give up. It's not an option. I remember having those moments when I didn't see the point in doing anything, but I kept moving on. Look at me now."

Every word she spoke was clear and distinct. She was delivering the message in deep tones that reached every ear in that room and everywhere else wherever the people watched her from. In my heart I believed that message was clearly for someone, Vera included. That was very enlightening.

She also pointed out that generally women struggle to be heard when they have been sexually assaulted for fear of being judged and blamed.

She went on to say, "You are not to blame when you are assaulted. You didn't put yourself in that position someone else did, but unfortunately, sometimes society has a different opinion. They blame the victim because of the way they were dressed, what they drank or whatever excuse they can come up with. There's no reason ever to justify sexual violence period".

She paced up and down quietly for about a few seconds and then she continued. "You have to release yourselves from a prison called unforgiveness. Despite what happened, you have to release these people from your heart. They don't have a place there. Forgive them," she said softly. "This is something you need to do to move forward. You don't have to forget what happened but forgiving plays a big part in the healing process and it's also a Godly thing to do. I can assure you that it's not easy, but it's a doable process. Remember you are doing it for you not them so that you can move forward."

Pastor Myranda concluded her speech with a challenge. "Are you ready for the next chapter of your life? I know I am talking to someone whether you are here in this room or you are watching me from wherever you are. Are you ready? Pick up that mat and start walking. Find yourself again and live your life as God intended. Don't let the hurt or the pain stop you from being who you are, because you are someone. Don't let whoever put you in that comprising position continue stealing from you. Believe it or not, good things still come out of our pain and hurt. It is your responsibility to get your life back, and there's no better time to start than now. Nothing is impossible when you believe and commit".

I liked everything about that pastor. She had done a good job delivering her message with power and panache. The room went wild with applause. I found myself clapping too.

In some parallel existence, I could hear Vera. From the day she shared her story with me, I couldn't shake that image of her crying in that patients' day room at work. I never looked at her the same again. I realized that by opening up to me, Vera was hoping or expecting something from me. Maybe some advice, sympathy, anything I could offer. The truth is I didn't know how to respond or what to do except to make myself available when she needed a shoulder to cry on. I became her first and maybe only call for help. Her scars were scars on the outside, but inside the wounds were fresh and still bleeding.

The more I thought about my role in her life, the more I realized that although my heart was in a good place, I wasn't helping her move forward. The truth was pushing its way into my mind. It took that long for me to realize what I was doing wrong but, I was glad that I figured it out. I had encouraged her with the pity parties. When she cried, I cried with her. While it was okay to empathize with her, I needed to help her move forward.

So, after listening to pastor Myranda speak on television, I decided Vera needed to hear her, and maybe she could get something out of it. That was helping her differently, a way I had not thought of before.

I invited Vera to my house one evening on both our days off. She had been there a few times before. When she settled down, I offered her a drink. She wanted water instead. She drank deep and sat the glass down. We settled into a relaxed conversation. Vera never ran out of something to say. I then told her briefly what I wanted her to watch and that if she felt uncomfortable, we would stop any time. She listened attentively as the pastor spoke, her facial expression not changing.

When we finished watching she didn't say anything. I didn't say anything either., I waited for her to comment, but she didn't. The silence dragged on for a few minutes. I was uncomfortable, I kept telling myself that I was only trying to help, and that was the truth. I fought the temptation to look at the expression on her face. Was she angry, was she crying? I didn't want to know. I wanted her to say something; this was a sensitive issue. I had rehearsed what I wanted to say. I waited for her to start, but nothing was forthcoming, and then her cell phone rang. She moved away from me and walked towards the kitchen to take it. When she came back, she told me she had to go mentioning something about her husband locking himself out of the house. She didn't say anything about the pastor's speech. I gave her a knowing look. Then we-can-talk-when-you-are-ready kind of look. Then she left.

Vera never said anything when we met at work the following day or several days that followed. She acted as if that day never happened. For crying out loud woman, I was trying to help. She knew she could level with me, but she chose to be quiet. I decided to play along with her game and give her more time. If she was mad, I didn't understand why she couldn't just say so?

At the end of shift one Saturday, almost two weeks later, she surprised me when she asked me if we could go and have breakfast. I had a feeling she was ready to talk. I was ready too. We went to a small restaurant not far from work which I had never been to but heard they had good food. After giving our orders to the waiter, she started talking.

She started by thanking me for being that friend that was willing to listen. "My friend, you could have told me to shut up so many times, but you didn't," she said smiling. I rolled my eyes and smiled too. "More than anything I want to thank you for allowing me to be sad, not pushing me to get over it and for not giving me the false reassurances. … You will be okay, how do they even know I will be okay and what do they mean anyway…. I hate it when people say that. You are a good listener," she said.

Yes, I am, thanks to you, I thought to myself.

She added, "Sometimes words can heal, but at times just the silence does the trick. I appreciated the silence a lot. I wanted to be heard, without you commenting. Just a listening heart and ear and I got that from you."

Silence? For real! That was huge coming from an incessant talker like her!

"I am sorry I took so long in coming back to you. I went home and checked out the pastor's website," Vera said. "I listened to most of the speeches she gave on YouTube. There are different versions, depending on the audience, but the message is mostly the same." She paused and looked at me. I didn't say anything. Maybe the right thing was for me to say it was okay, no big deal but I couldn't bring myself to lie to her. It was a big deal because she had left me hanging for far too long. I just looked at her with a blank expression.

"She is a busy woman," she continued. "She speaks mostly to churches about sexual abuse. I watched several of her speeches on YouTube. It was after listening to her several times that I felt the urge to do something more with my life. It was like a fog had been lifted from my brain and I could think a lot more clearly because the fog was gone. Sad as it was, her story is captivating. One thing I learned was that what my future holds is greater than my past. I am ready to start the process of repairing my life, not covering it up like I have been doing. There's no point in dwelling in the aspects of my life I cannot change. I know I can never forget what happened, but I am hoping that, like pastor Myranda, I will someday get to a point where I can talk about it without breaking down. I have had these scars for this long; I might as well wear them proudly. I have already been through the worst and am about to make it to the other side."

"I admire your courage," I told Vera.

"Courage has got nothing to do with it." She looked down for a moment, then looked back at me. "What choice do I have?

"I have decided to talk to my pastor first, tell him my story for the first time. I know he will be shocked, and then I will let him know what I intend to do. Women out there are struggling to be heard when they get sexually assaulted, but they don't know how to go about it. For the most part, they don't want the world to know because they feel embarrassed about it like they are to blame. If the pastor allows me, I will start by talking to the people in my church. I know exactly how this feel."

I caught a note of hopefulness in her voice. I thought that was a good place to start. I didn't doubt she would do it, but a lot of people from her church would be surprised.

"I am still a bit unsure, but it has to be now or never." Her eyes began to well with tears. She wiped them away with the back of her hand. "I can't believe it's me saying this. For years I kept it to myself except for a few individuals I confided in, but now I am ready for the whole world to hear my story. I believe one or two people's lives will be changed as mine was by this pastor Myranda. I know my family will not be happy, but I wasn't happy for a long time, and no one stopped living."

I observed her as she spoke. She was looking straight ahead as if gathering her thoughts, but I could see the determination.

"I hope I will be able to deliver the message as effectively as the Pastor Myranda."

"Why not?" I asked.

"I believe God will use my circumstances to change someone's life as He did with Pastor Myranda. She changed my life. I am forever grateful for the impact she had on me. The way she spoke, the way she carried herself, pulled me in."

I didn't doubt for a second that she would. I told her that everyone was fighting some kind of battle, and I admired her for trying so hard to be always positive, at least on the outside. She was in pain and had pushed through for most of her life with a smile on her face all the time. That must have been tough.

We continued talking through our breakfast.

"I thank God for making our paths meet. Your friendship, wisdom, and patience, have been a guiding light in my life. Everything happens for a reason. I hope one day I will be able to return the favor, "said Vera.

We parted ways as she walked to her car and me to mine. She walked with a pleased-with-herself manner. She deserved it. It was high time.

I couldn't remember when I had last felt so satisfied with life. I was glad she had decided to take that route. She had a gift with words. Vera was a brilliant woman, and I didn't doubt that if she started to talk about her experience and encourage other victims out there, she would do a good job. That marked the beginning of a long healing journey in her life.

She would turn her adversity into Inspiration and Empowerment for herself and others.

Joyce Hativagone Damiso

Joyce Hativagone Damiso was born and raised in Harare, Zimbabwe. A graduate of Oklahoma State University, she is a Registered Nurse and has worked in this field for seven years. She started her career in the Health Field where she worked as a carer in the United Kingdom for four years before migrating to the United States of America. An entrepreneur at heart Joyce was also Chief Executive Officer for Raindrops Counselling services from 2014 to May 2018.

Even though Joyce has always loved to write, her career is just beginning as this is her first published story. She is currently working on more short stories and looks forward to publishing her first book before the end of the year.

One of her passions is reading mostly Christian and fiction books. She loves traveling which helps her connect with new people.

The Damisos are blessed with two daughters, a son and a grandson and currently live in Oklahoma City.

To connect with Joyce:

tyradrops3@gmail.com

https://www.facebook.com/joycehativagonedamiso

CPSIA information can be obtained
at www.ICGtesting.com
Printed in the USA
FSHW011749250419
57581FS

9 781989 035054